Return to

D0840876

DEAR GOD,
WHEN IS IT
MY TURN?

"You believed that God would do what he said; that is why he has given you this wonderful blessing."

Luke 1:45,
The Living Bible

DEAR GOD, WHEN IS IT MY TURN?

by Doris Moeller

Scandia Press
Indianapolis

Copyright © 1991
by Doris Moeller
All Rights Reserved

Scandia Press
P.O. Box 501405
Indianapolis, IN 46250-1405

SCANDIA PRESS
8060 CLEARWATER PKWY
INDIANAPOLIS, IN 46240-4903
ISBN 0-9629058-0-1

Preface

I offer this story in celebration of God's role in my life—His curriculum for my growth and discovery. I'm willing to share my personal struggle hoping it will encourage you in your own journey toward wholeness. I want you to know it's possible to change no matter how old you are.

My story is a search into feelings and memories. Studying the past helps me to make better choices in the present. Reviewing yesterday's relationships helps me to understand today's responses. I believe God is leading me in this process of learning. I believe He has a special purpose for my sharing it. God loves you and He will help you to examine your own life and the patterns unique for you.

I don't want divorce to be a focal point in this story. I want the focus to be on my personal transition. I do not believe divorce is required for healing. Maybe my narrative will help you avoid that tragedy.

I want to testify with my whole being that the rewards of growth are worth the struggle. I thank God for every step of the way—for every painful lesson. I marvel at the way He has intervened in my life. I'm still learning, but I'm on a steady course. No matter what happens, I am confident that God will never fail me.

Dedication

I dedicate this book to God and the people who have contributed to my growth and the quality of my life. They know who they are.

I am especially indebted to Robin Norwood for her book *Women Who Love Too Much*. When I read it, I understood my life for the first time. I followed her road to recovery and five years later, I am merrily on my way.

Contents

Preface   *v*

Dedication   *vi*

1   Formative Years   *1*

2   Following the Pattern   *13*

3   God Hears Me!   *21*

4   Old Patterns Hang On   *27*

5   Praying and Pondering   *37*

6   God's Mysterious Ways   *55*

7   Inner Search Begins To Focus   *65*

8   God Leads Me Away   *73*

9   Time Out to Face Reality   *77*

10   Learning New Ways   *99*

11   Back Home, Will It Be Different?   *119*

12   Another Move   *137*

13   Highs and Lows of Divorce   *157*

14   And The Learning Goes On   *175*

15   New Patterns At Last   *205*

16   The Big Picture   *237*

Epilogue   *245*

1   *Formative Years*

My family went to the seashore last week.
I think I had a fun time.
On the walk to the beach,
we passed a toy shop
with a wonderful dolly in the window.
I stopped to look at her every time we went by.
My family called to me
so I wouldn't be left behind.
"Throw your dolly in the ocean," my daddy said.
"If the waves don't bring her back,
I'll buy the one in the window for you."
Sometimes my sisters would help me
because they could throw farther than I.
I tried every day,
but my old rubber dolly always came back.
I still have her.
I brought her back home.
Did my daddy know
the waves would always bring her back?
If he knew that,
why did he tell me to do it?
Why did he let me try so hard?

ɜ ɜ ɜ

On our way to the ocean
we rode on a big ferry.
My sisters hid me
on the floor of the car
so we wouldn't have to pay as much money.
The blanket was hot and scratchy.
I could hear them giggling.

❦ ❦ ❦

We live in a square brick house.
Mother and Daddy are very proud of it.
I don't tell them
I think it's ugly.
My room is upstairs above the driveway.
Daddy goes to work late at night.
When I hear his car slowly pull away,
I get sad.
If he didn't have this house,
and all of us,
he could sleep like we do.
When my eyes are wet,
the hall light
has points like a big star.

❦ ❦ ❦

I have the measles.
My room must be kept dark.
I hear mother working
downstairs in the kitchen.
I wish she would be up here with me.
Maybe after school
my sisters will come up
to see me.
I don't like to be sick,
and I especially don't like
being sick all alone.

❧ ❧ ❧

On my birthday
my sisters gave me a box
wrapped like a special surprise.
Inside was a dead beetle.
They did it for fun.
They all laughed.
I'm trying to laugh too,
but I'm very embarrassed.
I don't want them to know
how disappointed I am.

❧ ❧ ❧

I wish I were grown up.
No one has time for little people.
There's nothing to do all day.
Sometimes I walk to Aunt Jennie's house.
She's always glad to see me
because she's old
and kinda crippled.
She lives with her son.
She stays upstairs in a little room
reading her Bible.
She teaches me songs
about joy in my heart.
"Don't bother her," mother says,
"she doesn't have time for you."
But Aunt Jennie's not working,
and she always seems
glad to see me.
She says I shouldn't go home so soon.
Why does Mother tell me that?
Is Aunt Jennie
really glad to see me?
How can I be sure?

ₐ ₐ ₐ

Today was the first day of school.
I wanted to go,
but I was scared.
My teacher is nice.
She gave us a paper
with a square and a circle on it.
We should color the square red
and the circle orange.
I cried
because I wasn't sure I'd do it right.
The little girl next to me
helped me.
I hope she sits beside me tomorrow.

ᵃ ᵃ ᵃ

We go to Sunday School sometimes.
I hate it.
When I get to the table where I belong,
the first thing I hear is:
"Where were you last week?
We didn't get the banner because of you."
I don't say anything.
It's not my fault.

ᵃ ᵃ ᵃ

When I grow up,
I'm going to have lots of children.
I'll read to them,
play with them,
take them to fun places.
I'll never be tired or sad.
I will always look pretty.
When I visit their school,
they'll be proud of me.
I will love them lots and lots,
and they'll know
how much I want them.
Other people will like them too.
My children won't laugh at each other
because I won't allow it.

                    ớ ớ ớ

My mother is a little woman.
At least she seems that way to me.
Her nose is tiny—her feet are too.
But her body is fat.
Maybe she seems little
because she is so mild
and never gets her way.
She works all day
except after lunch
when she takes a nap on the sofa.
Funny, that's when I like her the best.
She's peaceful then,
and her face looks soft.
Her hands are rough because she works so much.
I try to help her,
but it doesn't do any good.
When I help her with one thing,
she begins on something else.
Sometimes it seems like
she does things that don't need to be done.
I don't understand it.
When she's canning in the hot kitchen,
her face gets very red.
Her dress is all wet and worn in the front
where she leans against the sink.
I hate when she cans our food.
I don't like to eat it—not even the shiny peaches.

Sometimes Aunt Jennie comes to help.
She sits with a bowl in her lap
and pares peaches
while Mother fits them in a jar.
I like it when she comes,
except they talk in some funny language
that I can't understand.
I wonder what they're saying
that I'm not supposed to hear.
Aunt Jennie knows how to talk
like we do even though she wears
a long dress and a little white bonnet.
When we tease her
about having a bee in her bonnet,
she just smiles.
When I'm married,
I hope I can buy canned food
at the store.
No matter how hard I work,
I will look pretty for my children.
I don't want them to be sad
seeing me hot and messy,
my fingers all stained.

 る。 る。 る。

I'm finally teenage.
I wish I'd have someone to talk to—
someone who would understand.
When I talk to mother,
she doesn't get the message.
She doesn't hear it
like I mean it,
so I give up.
I come to my room
to be by myself.
I start telling her my hopes,
and end up listening to
her discouragement.
"Don't be in such a hurry to get married;
have fun while you can."
But my marriage will be fun.
I won't let it be dull drudgery.
I will do things better.
Anyway,
whatever happens,
I'll never tell my children.
No matter what,
I want them to think I'm happy.

ఇ ఇ ఇ

I yearn for a boy to love.
Being with him is all I want.
We'll walk in the woods on sunny days,
and plan our life together.
What kind of house we'll have,
and how many children.
What we'll do,
and where we'll travel.
We won't get caught in routine,
taking each other for granted.
I will love him so much,
I'll do everything to please him.
I will devote myself to him.
I will make him very happy—
then I'll be happy too.
I'll be special to him.
He will need me.

ૐ ૐ ૐ

I think I've found the man for me.
He is big, gentle, fatherly,
caring, warm, safe.
A medical student.
My friends say,
"You should play hard to get.
Don't jump up and run
whenever he calls at the last minute."
I think they're silly.
They don't understand
the quality of our relationship.
Why should I play dating games
when he cares about me?
Why should I refuse
when he needs me?
Why should I say I'm busy
when I'm waiting for him to call?
I don't understand their warnings.

&a &a &a

2 Following the Pattern

I'm married!
I am content.
We don't have anything fancy,
but I don't care.
Our apartment is in an old house.
Our first baby is on the way.
I can hardly wait.
I want lots of children—maybe six.
My husband isn't here much;
he's still getting his training.
By the time we have a big family,
he'll be home more.
I can't believe
I'm actually married
and truly belong to somebody.
All
   my
      dreams
        are
          coming
            true.

           ᔧ ᔧ ᔧ

We have just moved in with my husband's father.
His mother is in a mental hospital—
she has been there off and on since he was a child.
My husband is fired up to begin
a family practice in his hometown.
He has a new wife, new baby, but no money.
There's plenty of room for us here
with a washer and dryer I can use.
I'm trying to fit in, but it's strange.
Bureau drawers full of clothes
belong to someone I've never seen.
The furniture is drab and old-fashioned.
The young doctor eagerly takes calls
for older colleagues on vacation.
Sunday morning he goes to church with his father.
I stay home with our baby.
I'm trying to make the best of it,
but days get long in this dark house.
My baby is my escape—
this huggy little fellow is the center of my life.
My world has changed overnight.
The town has gained a new doctor.
A lonely man is reunited with his son.
I have a sinking feeling—
I'm losing a husband.

&a &a &a

I'm weary.
I shouldn't be—
we have our own home,
and I am truly grateful.
It's not big, but
it's in a friendly neighborhood.
We have four children—they are really sweet.
I love them so much.
My husband works long hours,
and I handle the phone calls.
On weekends I see other fathers
puttering in their yards and
playing with their children.
That's hard for me when I'm alone.
I plot to get all of mine
to nap at the same time
so I can sleep too.
I crave sleep.
I hear a cry.
Which child is it?
No matter—
each one is part of me.
I respond
twenty-four hours a day.

❧ ❧ ❧

Grandma is home from the state hospital.
A frontal lobotomy was done to modify her behavior.
As a manic-depressive,
she was either hyperactive and agitated
or too depressed to get dressed in the morning.
Years ago when she got out of control,
the sheriff would have to be called.
There would be an ugly struggle.
As a little boy, my husband watched.
Sometimes he would hide.
He doesn't talk about it much,
but I see what it has done to him.
I think that's why he works so hard—
he needs to erase his shame.
He wants the world to respect him.
Grandma is calm now—happy to be home.
She loves being with the children.
Each one is a delight to her.
I have become the daughter she never had.
My heart aches for her—how embarrassed she must be.
I wonder what she remembers, but I never ask.
Sometimes her eyes sparkle,
and her whole face lights up when she laughs.
She often talks about God.
His love is very real to her.

&ae; &ae; &ae;

My little girl is in a body cast.
We discovered her scoliosis
when she first tried to sit up alone.
As an infant, she had a strange illness.
She lay in her crib without moving.
I was terrified she'd have brain damage.
I pleaded with God.
Even though I'm pregnant again,
I can easily cope with her body cast.
This is nothing compared to fears I had.
I smock dresses
to fit over her solid form.
What a precious dolly she is
with her golden hair and big blue eyes.
She is such a happy little talker,
she charms everyone.
She lies perfectly still when x-rays are taken
and her cast is changed.
Sometimes when I watch her,
I think my heart will burst.
I'm so grateful there is help.
When we go for her check-ups,
we have a special day together,
just Janie and mother.
The boys stay home with a babysitter.

🐸 🐸 🐸

Dear God,
Thank you so much
for our new house,
the wide open spaces,
the peace,
the quiet.
There are no neighbor children
taunting each other
outside the bedroom window
when it's naptime for little ones.
Thank you for the serenity of aloneness.
I can't see other fathers playing with their children.
The world is far away.
My world is meadowlarks, fields, and sky
and me
and my children.
When I ring
the big iron dinner bell,
they come running home from the woods—
the little ones toddling along behind.
They look so cute.
I love it here.
Thank you so much.

&a &a &a

Janie is four years old today.
How will she blow out her candles?
She's flat in bed following a spinal fusion—
her dear little body encased in a clumsy plaster cast.
Her crib stands in the dining room
beside a large window—
no upstairs loneliness for this sweet child.
I propped an old table board across the rails
to hold her snacks and treasures.
Her crib is a center of activity.
We all take part—a baby gurgles beside her—
a toddler supplies toilet paper at bedpan time—
another holds up books.
When she first came home from the hospital,
my oldest son slept on the floor beside her crib.
I'll never forget his face as I carried her in.
Six years old, he solemnly held the door
as I maneuvered her through.
Story records play round the clock.
At night her tiny bell
beckons me to turn over the stack.
Rapunzel and Sleeping Beauty are part of our family now,
along with Bambi and Dick Whittington's cat.
I can hear her singing along.
She will have a happy birthday—
no dead beetles allowed at this party!

❧ ❧ ❧

Everyone has gone to school.
Even my littlest one is in kindergarten.
I guess I should be happy about it,
but I miss a toddler in the house.
A solid little figure squatting down
to reach blocks that topple off balance.
I miss a radiant ruddy face glad to see me,
chubby arms reaching up in excitement
as I walk smiling toward the crib.

ва ва ва

I'm going to have another baby.
My husband cannot believe it.
He just shakes his head
as I babble in anticipation.
Half in humor, half in desperation, he says,
"You've got to face it—
one of these children has to be the last!"
He remembers how difficult
my last delivery was.
I remember too, but I don't care.
I want to name him John.

ва ва ва

3 God Hears Me!

Dear God,
I am miserable.
I look out across the fields.
I search the sky.
Oh God, are You out there?
Do You hear me?
I brought this on myself.
I can blame no one but myself.
I schemed to have this baby.
I knew I shouldn't have him,
and I'm exhausted.
I can't cover it up anymore.
I'm worn out. It's all my fault.
If You don't help me,
I can't stand it any longer.
I am so tired.
Do You hear me? Are You for real?
I need help so badly.
I'm wretched of my own doing.
I'm at the end of my endurance.
If You don't help me,
I am finished.

❧ ❧ ❧

God!
I cannot believe it!
You heard me.
You *heard* me!
You are for real!
You *hear* me.
I know because I feel your presence.
I'm not the same!
Your love is so real—it is overwhelming.
I can hardly believe this is happening to me.
I am amazed that You hear me.
Who am I that You would listen to me?
Who am I that You would surround me
with Your Presence?
I stood at my window looking into the sky,
desperate for help,
calling out,
and You heard me!
Oh God, I'll never forget this.
Even if this peace fades away,
I will never forget it.
You hear me! You are here with me!
Oh God, I'm so grateful.
Thank you so much.
You hear me!

࿐ ࿐ ࿐

Dear God,
I'm waking up from my anesthetic.
I see Your cross on the wall.
Oh God, what would I do without Your peace?
My baby John.
Oh my baby John.
He is with You now, God.
Oh God, I know You love him
as much as I would have—and even more.
Oh God, thank you for the peace
You gave me just in time.
I see Your cross, the brass one on the wall,
and the wooden one on the hill.
I hear Your voice calling out,
"John, take care of my mother."
That was a different John—a man.
And now You have my John, my baby John.
I believe his life was for his mother.
He gave up this life
so I could know the reality of God.
He by-passed this life
so I wouldn't keep needing so many children.
Because now I know You, God.
I've learned You are really there
and You hear me.

ға ға ға

"Thou shalt have no other gods before me." [1]
But I did.
I had five
and I wanted six.
The chaplain asked me gently,
"Why do you need so many children?"
I handed him the letter from my mother,
mostly about cheesecake,
the recipe I had given her.
Her friends really liked it.
She hopes I am feeling better.
"Now I understand," he said softly.
He buried baby John today.
He and my husband accomplished it together.
My baby is gone, but
now I have you, God.
I've learned the first commandment.
I understand why it is first.
Knowing Your love is beyond description.
Your love is more precious than the dearest child.
It is more satisfying than cheesecake.

ba ba ba

It is almost two years since baby John died,
and now I'm facing surgery again.
A Caesarian section.
I'm allowed one last try.
I'm afraid to hope.
I have numbed myself for nine months.
I haven't picked a name.
I have not set up the crib.
I am suspended motionless
waiting for the surgeon to come.
The scrub nurse just said
to the circulating nurse,
"Have you ever seen anyone so calm?"
They don't know
I was awake all night
talking to You, God.
But I know
that You hear me
and You love me.
I don't *need* this last baby,
but I want him so much.

ཟ ཟ ཟ

"Mrs. Moeller, wake up.
Mrs. Moeller,
you have a little boy.
Don't cry so hard, Mrs. Moeller,
little boys are nice."
Oh my God,
she thinks I don't want him.
She doesn't know I'm finally free to cry.
I am free at last
to grieve for my loss,
to give voice to the pain.
The old chaplain has come to see me.
He is my faithful friend.
I hear him talking to the nurses,
explaining to them why I am sobbing.
I'm grieving for a little boy I never saw.
It's safe now to feel the pain.
My lesson is learned,
and this warm bundle is my fulfillment.
The psalmist says:
"Delight yourself in the Lord,
and He will give you your heart's desire." [2]
I believe it.
I will name him John.

4 Old Patterns Hang On

The benefit of Grandma's lobotomy has worn off,
and now tranquilizers modify her mood swings.
She spends a lot of time with us.
I undo long braids to wash her hair,
and fashion clothes for her large frame.
Sometimes I wish our children would have
a normal grandmother like their friends do.
I'm ashamed of my thoughts
when I see how much she loves them.
They are learning compassion.
Who's to say what's best for us?
They don't complain.
She gives them unqualified love,
and often tells them they have a lovely mother.
I think I'm the only one to notice
the change in my husband
when she visits.
Deep down
   I wish
      we could have
         Sunday afternoons
            alone.

      ða ða ða

My husband compliments me
about my appearance
and what I accomplish.
I am a good wife and a good mother.
He enjoys my company—I go everywhere with him.
When he makes housecalls, I wait in the car.
When he goes to the hospital, I wait in the car.
Waiting in a car with small children
is not easy.
I get angry at myself for choosing to go,
but again and again I repeat my mistake.
We want to be with him and it's the only way we can be.
It doesn't seem fair.
When I have somewhere I want to go, I usually go alone.
Why do I keep giving when there is little receiving?
Is it because he earns the money?
Is it because he is the head of the house
and we try to fit in with his plans?
Isn't that the right way?
But aren't husbands and fathers
supposed to give something besides money?
Am I expecting too much?
I honestly don't know how to find out.
Is this what my friends had in mind
when they warned me to "play hard to get"?

ào ào ào

Why am I such a fool?
I give in so easily,
it has become a habit.
I don't even know when I'm doing it.
I give in so graciously,
I fool everyone, even myself.
The resentment creeps in later.
That's when I recognize
I've done it again.
What's even worse—
I set myself up to be taken advantage of.
I volunteer
to do things for other people
I would not dream of
asking them to do for me.
I take on extra responsibility
before I stop to think.
My husband's needs
mean more to me than my own.
I slog along without complaining.
Why?
When will I stop?
What's wrong with me?
Will I ever learn a better way?
When is it my turn?

 za za za

I'm weary managing everything alone.
A friend, a motherly person, says:
"You have a big house, lovely children,
you are married to a fine man,
you can't have everything, you know."
She didn't have children—
she doesn't know how tired I am.
She doesn't have a beautiful home—
she couldn't guess what a mockery it is.
Belongings can't fill my emptiness.
How can I get her to understand?
Would anyone understand?
Trying harder only brings me more responsibility.
Does everyone struggle like this?
Am I expecting too much?
"It'll come," says my friend.
"It" never *"came"* for my mother.
I wish I wouldn't confide in her.
I feel worse after I do,
but I need to talk to someone.
I feel frustrated and guilty.
Where can I get good advice? What is fair?
I wouldn't mind working so hard,
if I were sure I'm doing the right thing.
I just feel so alone.

ᘒ ᘒ ᘒ

I overhear a conversation
coming from the kitchen.
A little girl
responding to her brother's taunts.
Unflinchingly, she counters,
"I know I'm right,
because
this is the way
Mother
does it."
Oh God, have mercy upon this little girl.

&. &. &.

Is it possible I have five teenagers!
How special they are to me.
Jane is vibrantly alive—a joy to behold.
The boys are steady and strong—
they work at a slaughter house.
I don't worry
about their getting into trouble.
They come home so tired,
all they need is enough food
and a chance to go to bed.
I love hearing them
laughing with each other.
Sometimes I feel bad—
I wish we would
take them on trips,
or have a lake cottage.
They are everything I want them to be.
I would like to give them more rewards.
I love them so much.
I want them to know
there is more to life than work.
Is there more to life than work?

ða ða ða

God,
I'm frazzled.
How can I get everything done?
Help me figure it out.
What do I do first?
What do I skip?
Everywhere I look
something needs to be done.
By the time I get the house the way I want it,
I'm too tired to enjoy it.
I'm like my mother
working, working, working.
I don't want to be this way.
God, what is the answer?
I don't feel right having someone clean for me
when I'm healthy and strong.
Besides, my husband hates outsiders in our home.
He had enough of that as a child.
There has to be a better way.
I'm determined to figure this out.
God, please show me what is right.

ᴓ ᴓ ᴓ

I have headaches for days at a time.
I wake up with them in the morning.
I feel like a war
is going on in my head.
Bright light hurts my eyes.
I can hardly stand noise or motion.
I comprehend what's said to me,
but it's difficult to grind out an answer.
My mind works in slow motion
as if my circuits are overloaded.
I hate being like this.
I feel like the children
will go to college and remember me
refuged in pillows,
not moving,
with pain on my face.
They don't complain;
they are lovely to me,
but I hate the thought of myself
looking so miserable.
This isn't how I want to be.

ða ða ða

Last week I had a hysterectomy.
I'm not bouncing back as fast as I'd like.
It's strange not being strong.
One minute I'm hot—and then I'm cold.
Getting special attention embarrasses me.
I think our timing was wrong.
My husband thought summertime would be good,
with everyone home from college to help me.
What a mistake—they're at work all day—
and I have eight people to cook for.

When I woke up from my anesthetic,
my oldest son was sitting with me.
I will never forget it.
I was miserable and he knew exactly what to do.
He sat there with his big hand on my arm.
"Mother, I know how sick you are," he said gently.
I will never forget it.
He was there with me.
He didn't need to do anything—he was just there.
That was enough for me.
Even though I couldn't move or talk,
I knew he was there.
I basked in that awareness
not wanting to miss a minute of it.

5 Praying and Pondering

I must have time alone
each day
to think things through.
My husband says I ponder the imponderables.
Doesn't everyone?
How do other people wrestle with ideas,
examine relationships,
read, talk to God?
Do they have a shortcut?
Do I have more to learn than they do?
When I talk to God,
the smog of weariness clears away—a heaviness is lifted.
I come alive.
I see the beauty of the day outside,
the coziness of my home inside.
I visualize those I love—
I commune with them right here in my chair.
In my spirit, I hug them.
I experience God.
I fill with joy.
I am inspired to try new things.
I have courage to begin again.

☙ ☙ ☙

It's not always easy to pray.
What prevents my meditation?
What gets in the way?
What keeps my spirit earthbound?
Do I get caught in the activity around me?
Heaven knows, it's busy here.
Is it too noisy to hear God's voice?
Am I self-conscious about praying
when someone else is in the room?
Am I afraid of ridicule?
Am I letting others overpower me?
Am I using them for an excuse?
When someone doesn't share my interest in God,
I feel uneasy and inhibited.
Am I influenced by things today
or leftover messages from the past?
I remember an experience when I was teenage.
I was in bed with a cold.
I thought it would be a good time
to read the Bible—
find out what it was all about.
No one in my family talked about God,
and I had the feeling we were missing something.
Something I needed. Something I wanted.
I thought I could read the Bible
like any other book
from front to back,
cover to cover.

So I began.
A formidable assignment to be sure!
I didn't get very far before
there was a voice at the doorway—
my father, asking what I was reading.
His reply to my answer was,
"Aw, c'mon, you're not that sick."
I felt foolish and embarrassed.
I didn't know what to say.
That was forty years ago.
Is that silly remark still echoing
or am I reacting to something else?
Is it possible?
My husband's mother often talks about God—
she's a mental patient.

⁂

When I'm with a silent person,
or someone who doesn't tell his feelings,
I suspect the worst.
He's thinking things he's not saying—critical things.
He doesn't agree with me.
He doesn't like what I'm doing.
In my discomfort, I do those very things.
It gets worse and worse.
Why am I so unsure of myself?
Why do I seek validation from others?
Why am I afraid of ridicule?
When I tell a story,
I include each detail
like I must document every tiny aspect.
What has been done to me?
When I was a little girl, I heard,
"That's all in your imagination."
"You're still wet behind the ears."
But that was long ago.
As a young wife, what did I hear
when I poured out my heart?
No one laughed or scorned.
I mostly didn't hear anything—
except maybe a murmur
or the rustle of the newspaper.

❧ ❧ ❧

When I reject an activity
because my husband doesn't want to do it,
do I stay home for his sake or mine?
Do I have courage to go by myself?
Have I been using him for an excuse?
Am I blaming him for being inflexible
when I'm actually taking the easy way out?
Am I reacting to old experiences again?
As a child,
I felt like I was on my own
with no encouragement or instruction.
I blundered along.
I wore an air of flippancy
to cover up how inadequate I felt.
I forced myself to venture out
to escape the void at home.
I wanted to learn better ways.
But now—now that I have my own home,
it's easier to stay where I'm secure.
Each time I send the children off to school,
I wave cheerfully to boost them on their way.
Inside I'm relieved and grateful
that I can stay home.
My years of challenge and grit are over.
I am safe.

࣌ ࣌ ࣌

Fashionable women
threaten me.
I feel awkward. I don't say much.
I am uncertain about the clothes I've chosen.
I'm self-conscious in those I've made myself.
I am homespun.
I would like to look expensive and sophisticated.
Maybe I do to others, but inside—to myself—
I feel like Little Orphan Annie.

      ᶻᵃ ᶻᵃ ᶻᵃ

Dear God,
I have a question about St. Paul's instruction,
"Be submissive to your husband." [3]
How can a woman be submissive to a husband
who is not home?
A husband who doesn't consider her needs?
What about an abusive husband?
An alcoholic?
I need to know—
I suspect many women need to know.
Was that instruction for long ago or today?

      ᶻᵃ ᶻᵃ ᶻᵃ

When I was a little girl, I adored my father.
I helped him drag branches cut from cherry trees.
I loved helping him. We were a team.
He made it clear what he wanted and I did it.
He praised me and we were both happy.
He took me with him to pay bills downtown.
He introduced me to his friends.
"This is the boss," he'd say.
I didn't feel like a boss—I felt like a princess.
Years later, as the confidante of my mother,
I saw him differently.
If only she had been able to defend herself.
If she could have told her feelings to him,
she wouldn't have stored up so much hurt—
the pain she unloaded onto me.
What torment I felt wanting to protect her
from someone I loved—from someone who loved me.
I was torn in two. I felt dishonest with each one.
I promised myself
I would never cause this conflict in my children.
I try to keep everything to myself.
It's a heavy load.
Some day will I get so filled up
that I will fall into the same mistake?
Is it a matter of time?

When can I tell
my feelings
to someone
who knows
how
to listen?
Someone who will
hear
what I feel.

I need someone
who will hear me,
but
not interrupt
to tell me
how I should feel,
what I should do.

I need someone
who will let me
learn
my own answers.

When will I learn
how to listen?
Merely listen.
Listen with my heart.

I've been a mother
for so long,
I interrupt,
I correct,
I advise.
I mean well.
I want to help.
I want to stop
your hurting.
Show you a better way.
I want to spare you
further hurt.

I need to
let you
learn
your own answers.

ಜ ಜ ಜ

Anger scares me.
Being angry with someone I love is awful.
Childhood anger brought disapproval,
    scorn,
        rejection,
            shame,
                anger from others.
It was better to be a nice girl,
    sit still,
        wait patiently,
            don't make a fuss,
                pretend it doesn't hurt,
                    hide the truth.
I did that—on the outside.
Inside I churned with conflict—struggled with resentment.
I felt deceitful,
    bad,
        guilty,
            miserable,
            alone.
I realize now I was incited to anger,
but not allowed to have it.
Anger still makes me shake inside.
It's a powerful force
that doesn't go away by itself—it just changes form.

                    ᣓ ᣓ ᣓ

It's New Year's Eve.
I'm sitting alone in the dark
watching the flames,
pondering the passing years.

What were the questions on my mind last year?
How were they answered? Has anything changed?
My husband is at the hospital
with a woman in labor.
How long can he continue to work so hard?
What is ahead for us?
What do other couples do New Year's Eve?
Are they happy?
Is there something
I should be doing differently?
What would it be like
to be married to someone else?

I'm remembering when I was little—
I sat beside my mother at the supper table.
One time I leaned over onto her lap
and she rubbed my face with her rough hand.
I can feel it this very minute.

   ❧ ❧ ❧

I wonder
how many women
fill emptiness with
fantasies of fulfillment.
Envision a face
and build a relationship
through day dreams.
Do they share
   feelings,
      longings,
         tenderness,
            with someone encountered only briefly?
I wonder
how many women
cling to a fragment of time remembered,
and expand it
into an everlasting source of energy.
Stimulating,
   enriching,
      comforting,
         tormenting.
I wonder if I'm the only one.

                    ð ð ð

Why am I attracted to men
of gentle dignity?
A soft-spoken, kind, quiet strength.
Does their calm manner
assure me of maturity,
deep feelings,
tenderness,
compassion for pain,
sensitivity for relationships,
capacity for joy,
spiritual perception?
Does a man's outward manner
give a reliable clue to how he is inside?
I want a man of substance.
I want someone who needs me for companionship.
Why do I yearn for such a man?
Why do I need his strength?
Am I reaching for the impossible?
Is there such a person?
Would he care for me?

&a. &a. &a.

Dear God,
I have a confession to make.
I'm not as loving
as people think I am.
My life has been hard
in ways I cannot tell.
When other people seem to have it easy,
deep down I am resentful.
Often when I listen to
someone else's experience,
I have an immediate flashback
of something painful in my own life.
It hurts all over again.
The bitterness seeps up to the surface anew.
I'm ashamed of my feelings.
I theorize, rationalize,
give myself a sermon.
But when I finish my discourse to myself,
I'm still hurting inside,
full of envy, resentment, or self-pity.
I can't admit this
to anyone, God.
It's hard enough
to admit it to myself.

❧ ❧ ❧

The past is not over—it's not behind me.
I might think it's finished,
but that's not true.
Old influences return in disguise.
The same forces appear behind new faces.
Struggles of years ago
often repeat in present day situations.
A small child stirs within me
with intense emotion.
I must learn to recognize when this is happening
and work it through.
It gets easier with practice.
I have questions I ask myself.
When have I felt like this before?
Who makes me feel this way?
I dig back further and further.
I write down whatever comes to mind.
What's the worst thing that can happen?
That usually solves the mystery.
Identifies the original experience.
How long will this happen to me?
Will it ever end?
Will time erase the pain?

ک&   ک&   ک&

Years ago I listened to my mother
ventilate what she did
for my father, my sisters, my aunts.
I did not understand then
that it was her way of validating herself.
It helped her to realize her accomplishments,
account for her activities,
cope with her choices,
soothe her pain.
I thought she was complaining.
I thought if I asked nothing for myself,
she would love me better.
I was wrong—
it separated me from her.
My independence created a wall between us.
That was just the beginning of my mistake.

As a student nurse I had an experience
I think I finally understand.
I shared the evening shift with a recent graduate.
I was terrified of my big assignment.
To bolster my courage
and establish a support system with her,
I offered my help to her in case she would need it.
In truth, I was asking for help I might need myself
but couldn't ask for.
Of course, she didn't recognize my hidden message.

How could she when I didn't myself?
Haughtily, she answered,
"Miss Snavely, I'm sure you have enough to do
with your own assignments—
how dare you offer to help me!"
I was dumbfounded. I felt sick inside.
I never meant to insult her.
My misleading approach made things worse than before.

That was thirty-five years ago.
I finally understand it.
I couldn't admit my fear even to myself
so I offered help to someone else—
help I really wanted for myself.
How many times have I repeated my mistake?
Offering a facade of strength to hide my fear.
The graduate nurse was insulted,
immediately fighting back.
I wonder how many other people
have been intimidated, diminished, offended,
without fighting back.
I wonder if anyone
has fought back quietly, passively,
deceiving us both.
My husband?

ᴢᴀ ᴢᴀ ᴢᴀ

Dear God,
I don't feel Your presence today.
I don't feel any sense of direction.
It's even hard to pray.
It's like my words come out
and fall on the floor
instead of going upward.
There is a dullness,
a deadness.
Fear and discouragement bog me down.
I hate it.
I'm glad I know this is normal.
I can't always be inspired and enthusiastic.
There have to be times of just hanging in there.
Isn't that what faith is—
believing when I don't feel anything?
I have to keep waiting and trusting.
I'll do today's work.
The blahs can't last forever.
I know how suddenly You spring the unexpected.
When You have a new direction for me,
I'll know it.
Please hurry.

ಶ ಶ ಶ

6 God's Mysterious Ways

Something is wrong—I'm not sure what.
I can walk to the mailbox,
but I have pain coming back.
I pretend I'm reading the newspaper headlines,
so I can stop for awhile.
Here's the strange part.
That old awareness of God's love, His peace,
His cushion of comfort surrounds me
just like it did before baby John died.
What is ahead? Why do I need this reminder
that I'm in good hands?

&a &a &a

It's twenty-one years since baby John died;
his birthday is tomorrow.
Twenty-one years since I learned God is real.
Since I learned I am real to Him.
And now I'm back in a hospital.
I've just had a myelogram.
I must stay overnight in case I react to it.
Everyone is very kind to me.

&a &a &a

Well, I did have a reaction to the test.
It was odd.
Whatever it was that happened,
occurred at almost the exact time
when baby John was born, and died,
twenty-one years ago.
Soon after midnight, June 6.
Isn't that strange?
It makes me shiver to think about it.
That's when God's love became so real to me.
His role in my life took on new meaning.
And now I feel like something significant
is about to happen again.
I've been in the hospital
for almost a week instead of overnight.
My room is spacious, cool, and still.
I am in pain. I must lie flat.
Everyone is delightful to me.
I can't get over it—I appreciate them very much.
My oldest son is a doctor here.
I depend on him like always.
I'm so proud of him.
His associates come to meet me.
I enjoy their visits.
I am content.

&a &a &a

I'm discharged until surgery next week.
I am staying at my son's house.
The timing is perfect.
My daughter-in-law is on maternity leave.
We have a lot to talk about—
what it's like to be a doctor's wife
and suddenly a mother.
This is a new experience for her;
and a special time for me.
What a lovely person she is.
The day goes fast.
I don't mind being sick at all.
It's ironic
how recently I reviewed
the death of my baby
and now this precious little boy
lies beside me.
What a panorama of life—
sorrow and joy,
pain and love,
loneliness and fulfillment.
How blessed I am.
Walking
is not the most important thing.

&a. &a. &a.

I've had surgery.
I'm in an orthopedic bed
with side rails and overhead bars.
Last night my son and his wife
brought their new baby to see me.
I was able to hold him
propped up in front of me—
his dear little form
seemed out of place in this environment.
His darling face looked so funny
peeking out from his wrappings.
He's a treasure.
What a treat for me to hold him.
I can't do much,
but it was easy enough
to smile at him!

&a. &a. &a.

Another son in this city
comes several times a day.
He announces the daily headlines,
crazy things he makes up about me.
He makes me laugh.
When he had croup as a little boy,
I held him in the night.
Now the tables are turned.
When he was born,
I went into shock for some reason.
I heard the nurse cry out in alarm,
"Call the doctor,
I can't get a blood pressure on Mrs. Moeller."
I thought I must be dying.
I didn't even care. I was exhausted.
Death seemed like a welcome relief.
I have not been afraid of death since then.
But back to the present—
that child is a man now,
standing beside my bed.
He looks so good to me,
I'm glad to be alive.
I don't mind being sick.
I'm not sick alone anymore.

‌ ‌ ‌

Is something else wrong?
I still cannot walk.
I should be able to by now.
My doctor is puzzled.
He can't understand it.
I think I do.
There is healing I need
more important than walking.
I think God is providing it.
My doctor is just the one I need
for this special healing.
He listens to me calmly.
I dread to tell him when something is wrong.
I wait for derision.
I never get it.
He has keen perception.
He gives me gentle answers with dignity.
I trust his competence.
I have never in my life felt so secure.
It doesn't seem important to me
whether I walk or not.
His eyes have a quality I can't explain.
He seems to speak with his eyes.
He hears exactly what I say.
Sometimes I wonder if
he hears more than I say.
He seems to be acquainted with sorrow.

I trust him
more than I have ever trusted anyone.
I know that God
has provided him for my healing.
One morning I answered his greeting,
"Oh, I'm just lying here meditating.
When you're a doctor's wife,
you feel guilty being sick."
He looked surprised,
but he said nothing—in words.
At the door, he stopped, smiled,
said quietly,
"Go back to your meditating."
I compare his response
to my dad's sarcasm years ago.
I thank God for him over and over.
Funny, sometimes we think
something has gone wrong,
when actually,
it has gone exactly right.
I'm not walking,
but I am healing
deep inside.

🙣 🙣 🙣

I am back home,
in bed mostly.
I'm not able to walk much.
I have a pleasant room.
I can see out the window
while I'm lying down.
The mock orange is blooming
in the side yard.
It is peaceful here.
It's good to be home,
but I miss talking
to the people at the hospital.
I miss my daughter-in-law.
I miss my sons.
I miss my doctor.
I think he really cared that I can't walk.
I don't admit to anyone
how much I miss him.
It seems strange to me
when I have so many other
people in my life.

ta ta ta

When someone is kind,
a tiny seed of safety
begins to sprout in me.
Leaves of trust begin to bud.
Warm expressions are sunshine.
Each gentle word is spring rain.
As time goes by,
I might even begin to blossom.
God created seeds.
He provides sunshine and rain.
He designs the blossoms.
He orders the seasons.
Spring comes after winter.

 za za za

7 Inner Search Begins To Focus

Sometimes my inner child of the past
takes over without a minute's warning.
Childhood fears overpower my adult reasoning
when I least expect it.
When I react to a situation
with inappropriate emotion,
chances are "my child is hooked."

When I returned for my medical check-up
able to walk without pain,
I could hardly wait to see
the doctor who had been so kind to me.
Since I had shared my need with him,
I wanted to share my joy with him.
I felt like a child
taking a surprise to a loving father.
Illness often revives one's inner child.
I waited my turn in a room full of people.
I talked to one person and then another.
The time passed quickly. I was not in a hurry.
I studied those across the room.
Suddenly I realized there were only two people left.
Two hours had passed—the afternoon was gone.
Panic seized me—what if my doctor had gone!

I would be laughed at for doing something stupid!
And then another realization rushed in—
eight weeks had gone by since my surgery.
My doctor had treated hundreds of people since then.
He wouldn't even remember who I was.
I was shaking as I inquired at the desk.
It was the secretary's mistake.
She apologized several times.
I was so relieved that it was not my fault,
I forgave her immediately.
Besides that, my doctor had questioned my arrival.
He did remember me!
I was so frazzled,
I hardly remember my actual check-up.
It took me hours to work it out—
the devastating impact of something so trivial.
I have finally learned that when I get to
the real reason—the big one—
I sob like a child. Then I know I've found it.
"Don't bother them, they don't have time for you."
How many times has this old tape undermined me?
It is my fault. I will be laughed at.
I'm only beginning to realize
the powerful effect these memories have had on my life.
Did God arrange the secretary's "mistake" for my good?

&. &. &.

I'm spending nine days with my father—alone.
My children used to be my support system
when I returned to this old house.
Why do I "walk on eggs" when I visit here?
I'm afraid to disagree with anything he says.
It's ridiculous.
I'm an adult with children of my own
and grandchildren too.
Why do I get hooked into childhood patterns
as soon as I come through the door?
My children are not afraid to disagree with me.
Why do I have this anxiety with him?
What's the worst thing that can happen?
How does a charming, gentle man instill such dread?
Maybe it's the uncertainty of never knowing
when his charm will turn to anger,
his mild humor turn bitter.
When his soft voice will begin to swear
suddenly for silly reasons.
He's unpredictable. I can't be honest.
It's better to keep flattering and agreeing.
But I hate that. It's degrading.
Why don't the grandchildren see this flip side?
They are devoted
to this jolly cardplayer and early-morning hiker.
I wish I could talk to my sisters about it.
They don't seem to be affected as much as I am.

God, help me with the answer.
What causes my stress?
Time drags.
I have trouble sleeping at night.
Everything goes around in my head—
old memories, new frustrations.
What is wrong?
He wouldn't ever hurt me.
He loves me. He is glad to see me.
What is tormenting me?
What is the worst thing that could happen?
Oh my God, I think I have it!
I think I have the answer.
His moody silence
goes on for days if we displease him.
He'll make it unpleasant for mother.
She is defenseless. He is unreasonable.
She cries. That makes him even madder.
She pities him because of his childhood.
He was the youngest of thirteen children.
He delivered groceries as a little boy.
He ran away and joined the army—
had his sixteenth birthday on the battlefield in France.
He sobs when there are newsreels of war scenes.
We've been taught to pity him, give in to him,
agree with him, cater to him, humor him.
It's the best way.

Otherwise, he will be nasty to mother.
If I speak up, she'll pay the price.
I'll be the cause of her abuse.
I'm afraid of creating a scene I don't want,
a situation I can't control,
a battle Mother is helpless to fight.
She can't leave—she must stay here with us—
she has nowhere to go.
Oh my God, she *is* gone!
She's been with you, God, for fourteen years!
I've been trapped in the past.
Mother, I've been trying to keep you safe,
and you *are* safe!
No wonder the grandchildren have a different view.
They don't get caught in this protective role.
Maybe my sisters don't either.
Do I finally have the answer? I think I do.
I'm free at last. Oh thank you, God.
Now I can relax and behave like an adult.
It's about time.
I'm free to leave—
whenever I need to, whenever I want to.
I'm free from childish fear. I'm free from anxiety.
I am free from the bondage of the past.
Am I really?

❦ ❦ ❦

I'm practicing something new.
Whenever my dad answers me with nonsense,
I respond quietly as though it makes sense.
It's pretty amazing—
instead of my being flustered,
and embarrassed, he is!
And then, I calmly leave the room.
I am free to leave.
I am proving it to myself.
I don't have to be a victim.
I've been working on this for several days.
It's getting easier all the time.
My heart doesn't pound anymore.
My knees don't shake.
As foolish as this sounds,
I'm very proud of myself.
In fact, I am exhilarated.
I *will* get free from the bondage of the past.
I can do it!

ﻌ ﻌ ﻌ

I remember the last time
I visited mother—
doesn't seem like sixteen years ago.
She had gotten so small—
she was curled sideways in an old wing chair,
her head nestled in one corner,
her legs held by the opposite arm.
The chair was like
a plump tender mother cradling her.
She was wearing a blue woolen dress
although it wasn't winter anymore.
The nylon quilted robe I brought her
was still hanging with the tags on.
I'm wearing it myself now,
wishing she had tried it on—
wishing she had discovered how soft and warm it is.
She was under medication for her pain.
She talked with her eyes closed—
a continuous litany of sorrow.
Many different names and events,
but the same mournful theme.
Each woman was a victim, taken advantage of,
and there was nothing she could do about it.
One time I protested,
"But mother, she could have said no."
"Oh no," she insisted,
"there was nothing she could do."

I did not interrupt again.
I just watched her as she talked.
It seemed to soothe her
to recount the tales.
She never paused from one story to the next.
I could see it was too late
for her to learn a new way.
I promised myself that
I would learn a new way
no matter how hard it is,
or how long it takes me.
It has been hard
and it is taking a long time.
I won't quit trying
until I change the pattern.
I am determined to break the chain.
I think I'm getting there.
Mother, I was right—there is a better way.
I wish both of us could have learned sooner.

&a &a &a

8 God Leads Me Away

I mourn for my husband.
I am horrified by what has happened.
I agonize over his coming home to an empty house—
our home in the country
where it was peaceful years ago.
The seedlings we planted are tall trees now.
The house, once full of laughter,
is silent.
The braided rugs remain—fabrics from old clothes
still recognizable in the twisted pattern—
a kind of chronicle.
The workshop is in order now—
the boys are gone too.
The wood lathe is still. Half-finished projects
have been cleared off the workbench.
Oh God, I can't believe this.
Has this really happened?
I always had his dinner ready
because he often missed lunch.
We ate as soon as he got home
in case he had to leave again.
Sometimes I met him at the door
with the message to turn back
to the emergency room or the delivery room.

Oh God, I can't believe this.
Has this really happened?
"Stop me if this is wrong," I prayed.
But You didn't stop me—
it was like You pushed me.
Sleepless nights, chaotic days,
driven along, doors opening for me,
everything falling into place.
Perfect timing.
All the while I was praying,
"God, I trust you,
stop me if I'm doing wrong.
Is this why You gave me
that cushion of comfort,
so I know You planned all this?
I couldn't bear it otherwise—
to me divorce is a form of violence.
I believe You led me here
to this apartment
that was vacated the morning I inquired.
I'm watching the sunset from my sixth floor window.
I'm looking over the city
where I came to school thirty-five years ago.
I see the park where I walked on my day off—
where I rejoiced in my expanded world.
Back then I was scared, but I welcomed the new freedom.
I can't believe I'm back at the same place.

I cannot believe I'm here by myself
after mothering six children.
I have come full circle.
What is ahead?
I cannot share the particulars
that led me to leave home.
I can only say
when God wants us to do something,
He knows how to get our attention.
He knows what will make us respond.
He leads us step by step.
How recently I reviewed my mother's life—
she was not free to leave.
And then God put this challenge in front of me.
Will I repeat the past
or learn from it?
Do I have enough courage to try a new way?

&a. &a. &a.

When God speaks to me,
He puts an idea in my head—
a strong impression that doesn't go away.
Sometimes I have a sense of urgency,
but I wait.
I don't force anything on my own.
God is in charge of my life—
He must prepare the way.
I ask Him to stop me if I'm mistaken.
I take the risk of embarrassment.
I trust Him even when I don't understand.
I'm trying not to guess His plans.
They are usually better than I could ever dream.
I promise to obey when He opens the door.
After I pass through,
often in suspense, sometimes in agony,
He gives me a special blessing.
I'm always glad I obeyed.
I am often amazed at what happens.
Awe and gratitude overwhelm me.
My faith deepens
to help me hear God's voice next time.

&a &a &a

9 *Time Out to Face Reality*

I can't be like a little girl forever,
frightened, trying to please.
I must grow up, stop kidding myself,
face reality. It's never too late.
If my needs are not being met,
why aren't they?
Why am I like this?
What can I do about it?

ءَ ءَ ءَ

I review my role as youngest child
in the shadow of older sisters.
I love these people—we laugh together.
Now it's easier for me to join in,
but I see why I fear ridicule.
I remember my embarrassment.
I understand my need to control;
it's safer than being subject to others.
I still fight old battles.
Only now I have a chance to win.
I can find new solutions.

ءَ ءَ ءَ

Looking back, the pattern emerges.
A little girl—
trying to please, not understanding.
A young wife—
wanting a better life, not knowing how to get it.
Too inexperienced to figure it out.
Striving to give children the very best.
I traded old unhealthy patterns
for new unhealthy patterns.
I shifted from helplessness to control.
From docile waiting to hyperactivity.
I went from one extreme to another.
Caught up in my zest for happy children,
I tried to be both mother and father.
I was willing to do whatever I thought it took.
Nothing was too much.
I was too busy doing it
to see the folly of it.

ᕽ ᕽ ᕽ

Dear God,
What is my part in this?
Please tell me what I'm doing wrong.
I want to face the truth.
How have I put out the message,
"Hurt me—I can take it"?
I've had enough hurt—I can't take it.
I don't want to invite any more.
What am I doing wrong?

≥a ≥a ≥a

I think I might see it.
I have been
slowly,
steadily,
committing emotional suicide
with massive overdoses of
caretaking and unselfishness.
Giving in.
Keeping the peace has been destroying me.

≥a ≥a ≥a

My life is making sense for the first time.
My husband is like the father that I outgrew.
My father told me exactly what to do;
praised me when I did it right.
He pruned the trees. I dragged the branches.
We were a team.
My husband didn't have to tell me what to do.
I already knew how to please.
He worked and I helped.
He praised me many times.
That's good enough, isn't it?
No. It is not.
Not when I have needs of my own.
Not when I need to share feelings
and be loved thoughtfully.
I need to receive as well as give.
I need equal partnership—honesty, openness.
I need adult companionship—
affirmation, understanding, tenderness, consideration.
Enthusiasm.
Surely marriage can be more than
helping with work.
That load gets heavy.
It is lonely.

ja ja ja

What happens when I live with
someone who resists change?
Someone who criticizes new ideas,
emphasizing the negative aspects.
Someone who squelches enthusiasm
silently,
quietly,
intellectually,
sarcastically,
explosively.
I lose my self-confidence,
hesitate to try new things.
Wanting to keep the peace—I keep the problem.
I get discouraged.
Afraid of anger, I store resentment,
become depressed,
withdraw.
Keep silent.
The foundation is laid for a defeating lifestyle.

❧ ❧ ❧

When someone is closed to communication
how do I feel?
When someone is threatened by questions,
not wanting to see himself honestly,
I become wary—I draw back.
Some people actually invite me to lie to them.
I deceive instinctively,
evade certain issues,
do things furtively to avoid conflict.
Integrity is not worth the risk.
I'm afraid to tell my feelings.
I hide behind a mask
and postpone confrontation as long as I can.
I stall until the situation is intolerable.
Even then I don't want to face the truth.
I try not to feel.
I deny anything is wrong.
I need help—I don't know I need it.
I want it—I don't want it.
Stuck deep in this milieu,
I become accustomed to it.
How do I feel?—I don't feel.
I get desensitized.
Numb.

ン ン ン

"If you tell her, she'll give up.
Do you want to kill her?"
My dad bound us to secrecy.
We made daily excuses for Mother's vomiting.
"There's a bug going around. The pizza was too spicy.
Next time we won't order green peppers."
What a nightmare it was.
We played a game of gaiety—nothing is wrong.
I just dropped by (from 600 miles away).
My high school reunion was a good excuse.
An old classmate of mine, one of her favorites,
visited her and played along.
If we played our game too well,
my dad would feel sorry for himself,
"You don't care how tough it is for me."
What a no-win situation.
We all played—even my mother.
She threw up while Daddy was in the basement.
She'd gag herself to get it done
because it upset him to see her sick.
After three years of deceit,
my food-loving mother
weighed eighty-eight pounds and died.
I wasn't there.
I didn't stop by on the right day.

꿈 꿈 꿈

God does not endorse denial. God is truth.
He wants the truth to set me free.
He knows how to get my attention.
When I'm in denial, I often have physical pain.
Pain that doesn't come out of my mouth
goes somewhere else.
My turmoil comes to the surface one way or another.
In a heart-wrenching situation,
I have pain in my chest.
If there's a war going on in my head,
I have headaches.
If there's too much to take in,
I have difficulty swallowing.
If there's something I reject,
I am nauseated.
I would rather substitute physical illness
than admit I have a problem.
It's a form of wishful thinking.
Doctors will cure me if I am sick.
If I admit I have a problem in my life,
I will have to figure it out, make new choices.
I get more support with physical illness.
I'm not ashamed to ask for it.
Sickness is respectable. I will be loved.
But, I might as well face it—my problem won't be solved
until I admit I have it.

❧ ❧ ❧

When I deny reality,
I don't consciously lie to myself.
It's deeper than that.
I simply cannot bear to face the truth.
Honesty is too painful—
the disappointment is too great.
My dreams are shattered.
I am afraid. I am ashamed.
Sometimes we hear people cry
"Oh no!" as they face a tragedy.
Denial is an instinctive protection
against the shock of truth.
I can deny something
when the facts are right before me.
When conflict is subtle,
I can overlook it for a long time,
maybe years.
I've been trained to disguise unpleasantness,
to conceal disharmony.
"It's all in your imagination."
"You think too much."
"How can you say such a thing!"
I can be blind to a situation
that is obvious to someone else.
I fool myself.
Sometimes I am too proud to face the truth.
What would I have left?

How could I carry on?
What would people think?
The consequences seem so terrible,
I put off looking at reality.
I rationalize—make excuses.
I am uneasy and scared.
I am embarrassed.
The funny thing is
once I decide to face the issue,
it's a tremendous relief.
The pain of the truth
is not as bad as
the pain of confusion and denial.
It is different somehow.
It is a clean wound,
not festering underneath
with dread and uneasiness.
The hurt is out in the open with a chance to heal.
I can share honestly with others
and receive support.
I will feel lighter, free,
able to move on to a solution.
I have new energy.
I can think about other things again.
I can sleep at night.

&a. &a. &a.

We are a dysfunctional family.
My husband is addicted to work.
I'm addicted to making him happy.
He is a workaholic.
I am the enabler
allowing him to keep striving.
The world is impressed.
My husband is successful.
I am the woman behind him,
supporting him
    encouraging him
        managing his house
            raising his children
                meeting his needs
                    and everyone else's
except mine.
The world does not recognize
our family is out of balance.
It is pathologic.
It is sick.
It is contagious.
The children are part of it.
The impact has already been made.

                   ও ও ও

I must say it again out loud.
We are a dysfunctional family.
We are *all* part of it.
Some recognize it. Some don't.
It is frightening.
Confusing.
It's a shock.
It's a relief to admit it.
We will need honesty.
We will need help.
We will need courage
and determination to change.
People won't understand.
Some in the family will be angry,
hurt, puzzled, resistant.
Some will gloss it over.
Deny.
Ridicule.
Scorn.
That's not my problem.
I must say it again.
I must say it until I believe it myself.
I am part of a dysfunctional family.
There is help.
I will get it.

☙ ☙ ☙

"She's an enabler."
What does that mean?
Enabling means helping someone else
to follow his chosen course more easily.
Being an enabler means to me:
loneliness,
responsibility, hard work,
disappointment, fear,
fooling myself, making excuses, covering up,
embarrassment, hurt pride,
dreaming of better days,
never giving up hope,
trying harder,
frustration,
exhaustion,
depression.
When I finally realize
that I have given all my energy
to enable someone
to do the very thing
that has caused me so much pain,
I feel anger.
PURE VIOLENT RAGE.
Deep down under all that rage
is unspeakable sorrow.

࿐ ࿐ ࿐

What happens when the enabler
needs encouragement?
What happens when this strong pillar
begins to sway?
Where do I find someone to lean on?
Is this when I recognize
the role I've been playing?
Is this when I realize
I'm not strong at all—
I am merely addicted to struggle.
I realize my programming was set up long ago.
Keep waiting.
Keep smiling.
Don't complain.
Try harder.
Keep going.
It isn't working anymore.
I'm tired of pretending.
I want help.
The psalmist said,
"I will lift up mine eyes unto the hills,
from whence cometh my help." [4]
He was right.

ᶻᵃ ᶻᵃ ᶻᵃ

Being an enabler isn't too great.
But giving it up
is the pits.
Life is empty—there's no purpose.
I have so much love to give,
but no one to give it to.
I need my new freedom,
but my sorrow is overwhelming.
I can't concentrate on what I'm doing.
Life seems meaningless
without someone to do things for.
Hollow.
I must learn my lesson.
I must not replace my old "fix"
with a new one.
I must suffer the withdrawals
for the sake of freedom.
My freedom.
Wholeness.

ᏧᏧ ᏧᏧ ᏧᏧ

Now *I'm* doing it!
I'm making the same mistake!
I know the dysfunction I've had
because my mother told her pain to me.
And now—what am I doing? That very thing!
I'm pouring out my anguish to my daughter.
Oh my God, help me to stop!
She's not as young as I was.
Will that make a difference?
She's already married.
Can she learn from my mistakes?
Am I being open and honest or destructive?
She's very kind to me. Supportive and caring.
She remembers hearing my crying
after she was in bed at night.
I guess I wasn't as clever as I thought.
Now it's out in the open—no more secrets.
I'm finally telling my pain.
Maybe the important thing is what I do
to stop spilling my overflow.
Maybe I can still break this chain of dysfunction
for the not-so-little girl
who trusted the way mother did it.
I hope we learn new patterns together.
I hope it's not too late.

ৰ ৰ ৰ

Underneath my air of calm
is aching emptiness.
I'm realizing my hopes
might be idealistic fantasy.
The intimacy I long for might never come.
I tell myself
the years were not wasted.
I learned many lessons.
I began friendships that I cherish.
I came to know God
through loneliness and desperation.
I'm lonely now
without my illusions.
But I'm not desperate.
I haven't lost God.
He's not idealistic fantasy.
He is tested reality.
I will keep holding on.
I'll wait to see what happens.
It's not easy.

&. &. &.

When I'm restless,
uncertain, weary,
it helps me to pinpoint the reason.
Today I'm in limbo.
Simply that.
I'm between frantic activity and what comes next,
but I don't know what that is.
I'm waiting for directions.
I have no idea what is ahead.
Being in limbo is unsettling and depressing.
I must be honest about my feelings.
I am uneasy, and probably scared.
My life is strange now.
There are no pressing commitments.
There is no backlog of work to be done.
My disconnected thoughts rattle around
in this empty schedule.
Maybe I can use the respite—
a time-out to enjoy some things
I couldn't fit in before.
I must make the effort.
I keep a list of ideas for days like this,
days when I have the blahs—days when my spark is out.
I just have to get started on one of them
for my engine to get running again.

ᵛ⃘ ᵛ⃘ ᵛ⃘

When a man is mild-mannered,
I may not recognize he is manipulating.
Controlling. Passive aggressive.
I think it can't be—I must be wrong.
But it can be.
When a man is jovial, fatherly,
I can't imagine the world of feelings
is dead to him. Buried.
But it can be.
When pain is deadened, joy is dormant too.
Life is wooden. There's no resonance,
no ringing clarity, no lightness.
A negative spirit flows underneath.
Life journeys along
emphasizing food and routine chores.
There is humor, but, somehow it's not refreshing—
it's often sarcastic, derogatory.
I feel restless. Suffocated.
I am puzzled. I don't know what is wrong.
I don't trust my perceptions.
There's no one to ask.
I don't know what is missing.
The discord is subtle. Evasive. Passive.
I don't trust my judgment.
Soothed by a warm voice,
I miss the underlying message—the hostility.
I may deny and make excuses for a long time

before I finally face reality.
Sometimes I become so confused,
that only God can lift me out.
He can save me from a dilemma that
I cannot figure out.
That is what happened to me.
God was able to lift me out
because I turned to Him years ago.
I trust Him.
He could lift me out
because I trusted Him enough
to obey in blind faith.

&a &a &a

Bound by my old family patterns—
shackled, too, by my husband's history,
I was twisted into a double knot of pathology.
No wonder God led me out—
He sets the captives free.

&a &a &a

I mustn't look to another person
to bring me fulfillment.
I, alone, must learn to fill my emptiness.
I must establish a sense of purpose for myself.
Caring for a family was an obvious purpose,
easy to identify and accomplish.
But now—what now?
I will overcome my patterns of denial,
and face life as it is.
I am determined to do it.
I want to be finished with poor communication.
I will address an issue openly and honestly.
I will seek answers to my questions.
Learn to solve problems objectively.
I will build new relationships.
Strive for balance in my life,
learn to receive as well as give.
I will seek wisdom.
I already know that
wisdom begins with trusting God.
I've been doing that for a long time.
He has brought me this far.
He will lead me further and further.
God will never forsake me.
This is reality.

❤ ❤ ❤

10 Learning New Ways

All of a sudden I am old.
The face in the mirror
has brown spots.
The veins on my hands
are a fascination
to probing little fingers.
How is it possible
for the shell outside
to be so far along
when the spirit inside
is just coming alive?
What a paradox
that words are harder to remember
just when my heart is bursting to speak.
How ironic
that days are dwindling
when there's so much I want to learn.

❧ ❧ ❧

I did not feel valuable
as a person.
I had to produce.
I had to serve.
I had to be nice,
make others happy.
Have a purpose to justify my life.
God is showing me
I am special to Him,
just me,
simply being alive.
I am valuable to Him
whether I am sick or well,
active or still.
Merely *being*—
being *me*.
That's enough for Him.
The other things are good,
but they are extra—
after the essential fact
of my being.
My being alive
is important to Him.
I am one of His sparrows.

2a 2a 2a

If I wait for my family
to understand what I'm doing,
I won't make any progress.
I must keep learning and changing
despite them.
It's not easy.
It is lonely.
I'm often afraid.
I must learn self-confidence.
When God leads me to do something,
I must not search for validation
from others.
If I believe in something,
and I'm aware of guidance,
that must be enough for me.
When Noah obeyed God
and built an ark,
He did not wait nervously
for his family, friends, and neighbors
to smell rain.
He had to begin.
So do I.

❧ ❧ ❧

Before when I was hurting,
and no one seemed to care,
I denied my pain.
To be in despair alone was terrible.
Deep inside I wanted to die.
To go on, I talked myself out of the pain.
Gave myself new promises of hope.
Set new deadlines of expectation.
Now I am learning
I won't get relief from pain
until I admit I have it.
I must let myself *feel* those things
I've locked away.
I'm beginning to do that.
God, You hear me, don't You?
You hear me sobbing.
In a bit, I feel better.
I am quiet inside.
I can go on.
It's important to tell painful memories
to someone else.
The freedom of release
is worth the agony of exploration.
Eventually, I will heal inside.

ða ða ða

Let me be honest—
I want to learn the truth about myself.
If you try to change what I'm saying,
it's hard to go on.
When you say
"Oh, you don't mean that"
just when I'm getting the courage
to reveal myself,
I must struggle to continue.
When I have to
convince you
that what I say is true,
I give up telling my story.
Please let me be honest—
don't encourage my denial.
I've been doing that
long enough.

ᔫ ᔫ ᔫ

Pain,
muffled,
screams for attention
somehow.

ᔫ ᔫ ᔫ

When I'm trying to work something through,
it helps me so much to share with you.
I don't need discussion
as much as I need your patience.
My words might not come out right at first.
If you argue in defense
of the other person involved
or give solutions I'm not ready for,
it slows down my process—and my progress.
A debate confuses me.
I am thrown off by your challenge.
I get side-tracked trying to convince you.
I feel frustrated, misunderstood,
wrong, guilty, rejected.
I am fragile right now.
If I hear scorn in your voice,
I won't be able to go any further.
I'll withdraw into silence to protect myself
instead of digging out what is wrong.
That's what I must do first.
If I have your support,
I can move on.
I might even see for myself
the very thing
you were trying to show me.

≈∂ ≈∂ ≈∂

You are very important to me.
I want to tell you my feelings
so you'll know who I am and what I'm about.
I'm willing to work on it. I need more practice.
I'm finding out that first telling my story
to someone other than you—
someone not directly involved—
is a good idea. It's safer.
I can sort through things
without fear of disagreement.
When I say things out loud, I can hear myself.
If I have it wrong, I can change it.
Talking to someone I trust is a rehearsal
so that when I share with you, I'll be ready.
I want our exchange to be productive.
I yearn for you to understand.
I'm trying to say exactly what I mean—
no mixed messages.
I want to be accurate—not ramble or generalize.
I don't want to bring in unrelated material.
I'm trying not to intellectualize.
I've been faking my feelings for so long,
it's hard to report honestly
what is happening to me.
But I'm trying and I think I'm getting there.
Please will you help me?
Will you try to understand me?

☙ ☙ ☙

I used to have the same dream.
Something bad was happening to me.
I never knew what it was.
The vivid part was
I couldn't call for help.
As hard as I tried,
I couldn't get any words out.
Even in my sleep I knew
if I could just make a noise,
a tiny squeak,
my husband would wake me up.
It took tremendous effort.
The sequence was always the same.
It was the only recurring dream I ever had.
Here's the strange part.
Now that I'm able to share
with people who listen,
I don't have that dream anymore.
I don't need to be rescued
from some unknown danger.
Could it be that our greatest danger
is not being able to tell our feelings?

 za za za

I'm trying to be a good listener.
Especially for you—I love you.
When you're talking to me,
I don't want to react
to what you say before you finish.
When you attack me
in anger or frustration,
I jump in to defend myself
before I realize it.
I wish you would have someone
to help you sort things through.
I don't want the responsibility
you're trying to put on me.
Playing therapist for you
when I'm struggling myself
is a bad idea.
I wish I wouldn't try.
I'm not smart enough to recognize the games.
I get caught in them myself.
I feel pulled in two directions.
I want to help you—I get hurt myself.
I don't want your flippant sarcasm
to bruise me.
I'm bruised enough already.

ھ ھ ھ

When you challenge me,
I feel weak and almost sick inside.
I try not to let it show
because I want open exchange.
I want dialogue with you.
I push myself to ask questions,
and urge you to continue,
but I feel hollow inside.
A simple difference of opinion
is enough to threaten me right now.
I'm acutely aware of how wobbly I am.
I hate being so vulnerable—I want to toughen up.
I know I need correction—and I do want to learn from it.
But I ache for encouragement—
I need it to keep going.
It is my invitation to live.

 za za za

I'm learning to be careful when I share.
I'm beginning to notice
when someone's response is determined
by what is happening in his own life
rather than what is happening in mine.
I'm starting to recognize
when a listener projects his own attitude onto me.
That makes me uneasy.
I'm afraid I'll be misquoted.
I'm becoming more selective.
I hope I'm getting wiser.

ﬠ ﬠ ﬠ

I want to build myself up,
but I can't do it by running others down.
I feel ugly afterwards.
As I confide my story,
let's not condemn the one who hurt me.
That fills me with conflict
and I'm sad enough already.

ﬠ ﬠ ﬠ

Anger is like a lid
covering a box of other feelings.
Sometimes I can't get to the other feelings
without first lifting
the lid of anger.
The longer I sit on the lid,
the worse it gets.
Stored anger turns into resentment.
"Don't let the sun go down upon your wrath" [5]
means don't let another day go by
without opening the box.
Get to the feelings inside.
Allow yourself to be angry.
Start the healing process.
It helps me to have someone who lets me practice.
Someone who understands that
anger is a feeling I must work through.
I can't forgive until my hurt is out.
I might sincerely want to, but it doesn't last.
When someone helps me to *tell it all,*
and loves me anyway,
I am deeply grateful.
It is wonderful.
It is new life!

&. &. &.

When we moved into our new house
I painted a verse on the utility room wall.
I carefully lettered
"Your care for others
is the measure of your greatness." [6]
I quoted it from the Bible
and I believed it to be true.
For twenty-nine years
I loaded the washer and emptied the dryer
beneath those words until
I nearly destroyed myself.
My care for others
became the measure
of my sickness.
God has shown me my mistake.
In doing so much for others,
I neglected myself.
Surely that wasn't the way
He intended it to be.
I can care for others
and learn to take care of myself too.
That's a more healthy balance.
Those words on the wall were good,
but not to the extreme I took them.

ॐ ॐ ॐ

Whenever I read
in self-help marriage manuals,
"Don't expect your mate to change;
you must change first,"
I felt defeated and wrong.
There's nothing wrong with him.
I'm expecting too much.
I'm not a nice person.
I must try harder.
How could I try any harder?
But I always did.
Now I see—changing for me was not
trying harder to please,
taking on more responsibility,
expecting less for myself.
That wouldn't be any change at all,
but simply more of the same thing!
I must *change*.

ᨠ ᨠ ᨠ

I'm learning to be "selfish"
It is hard for me.
It has a bad sound.
Self-preservation sounds better.

ᨠ ᨠ ᨠ

I am responsible for myself.
Only I can work on my life
 to expand and grow,
  cope with problems,
   relate to others.
I am working to be independent
 emotionally,
  socially,
   financially.
I must keep a balance.
I need to share time with others,
 but not lose my alone time.
I want to meet new people,
 but not need others too much.
I must have caring supportive communication,
 but lighthearted fun as well.
I must plan future events,
 but take one day at a time.
I must be persistent in my efforts to change,
 but not be in a hurry for results.
I must allow myself to make mistakes.
I must become a loving parent to myself.

꿍 꿍 꿍

As a little girl,
I tried to protect my mother—
an unfortunate mistake.
I was powerless to do it.
As an adult, I took care of my mother-in-law.
She needed me—she wasn't well.
As a mother,
I supervised my children.
It was my job.
Since they are adults,
I must give up responsibility for them.
That has been easy for me
because they like to be independent.
I always encouraged them to be.
My husband is an adult.
I am not his mother.
I am not responsible for him
or his choices.
I must give up protecting him.
It seems ridiculous
that I have to learn that.
But I do,
and it's hard.

ₑₐ ₑₐ ₑₐ

When you overpower me
I don't like it.
When you do something
for me
that I can do myself,
it is demeaning.
I feel like a child.
When you take
my choices away,
sweetly, graciously,
I am frustrated.
When you give me advice
that I don't want,
I know I can figure
it out myself.
I get angry inside
and I don't like you.
When you make
judgments, not knowing
the whole story,
I feel frantic
because I'm not free
to tell the whole story.
I try to get away
physically or
emotionally.

When I overpower you
I don't realize it.
When I do something
for you
that you can do yourself,
I think I am kind.
I feel like a nice person.
When I take
your choices away,
sweetly, graciously,
I mean to be loving.
When I give you advice
I think you want it.
I think I'm saving
you added struggle.
I'm sparing you
because I like you.
When I make
judgments, I think
I understand
through my experiences.
Your emotions are mine.
Your problem is mine.
I want to help you.
I want to be needed—
that fills my need.

When I'm with someone
who shows any sign of stress or weariness,
I think it's my fault.
I talked too much, annoyed him in some way,
stayed too long.
Ah yes, they don't have time for me!
I don't consider any other circumstances.
As I'm learning to trust the love of others,
I want to be less critical of myself.
I want to replace old negative feelings
with more accurate messages.
I need to allow myself to make mistakes.
I must forgive myself when I do.

a. a. a.

I've begun a process
that will take a long time—
an ongoing process of learning new responses.
Finding new ways through trial and error.
Starting over.
Admitting mistakes, and then making them again.
Forcing myself to keep trying—keep hanging in there.
Listening to my inner voice—
tuning out the voice of the world.

a. a. a.

When I don't feel loved by you,
  it's hard to receive from you.
When I don't love myself,
  it's hard to receive at all.
When I don't love myself,
  I may defeat the very thing I want from you.
When I want loving attention from you,
  my behavior may keep you from giving it to me.

🐦 🐦 🐦

I understand now.
I must love others
as myself,
not
more than myself.
In order to love others
in a healthy way,
I must first be able
to love myself.
I will get my turn
when
I allow myself
to take it!

🐦 🐦 🐦

11 Back Home, Will It Be Different?

Dear God,
Thank you for the last nine months.
Thank you for all I've learned—
I want to practice those lessons.
Thank you for bringing me home—
help me want to be here.
Thank you for leading me away
to find my identity.
Please don't let me lose it again.
Show me how
to combine independence with togetherness.
Balance individuality with coupleship.
Be one *and* part of two.
Find a place especially for me
so I can be alone with my thoughts and feelings,
undisturbed and free.
A separate place for You and me.
Help me not to give up my turn again.

ಜ ಜ ಜ

My husband must choose his own response.
I can't do it for him.
I want us both to find out
it's safe to tell feelings—
much safer than holding them in.
I can't force him to make the transition.
He doesn't like change.
I hope we've learned the danger
of half-finished arguments—
issues brought to the surface,
and stuffed back under in unspoken truce.
We know the damage caused by storing anger,
but will we be able to let it out?
Will we have the courage?
I understand why God led me away.
We had lessons to learn.
Did we learn them?
Will we have a new start?
Will we have a new spark?

ðæ ðæ ðæ

What does sexual love have to do with intimacy?
It can be the perfect fulfillment
following a lovely time of sharing.
Sometimes it seems like just the opposite—
a substitute for communication.
Can sex be a form of denial—a cover-up
for a shallow relationship?
Physical attraction doesn't prove compatibility.
We might just be hungry for love!
Physical union doesn't replace caring,
communication, and loving tenderness.
I don't like the feeling that I'm being seduced.
I believe sexual love is meant to be
a special expression of deep mutual love,
but I'm afraid it's often
the battleground for a power struggle.
Arguments about sex are a convenient scapegoat
for those who don't want to work on deeper problems.
God surely must be disappointed
when we misuse His special gift.
I know I am.

ᜒ ᜒ ᜒ

Dear God,
Don't let me suffocate in dust and clutter.
My spirit is choking in endless chores.
What tasks are mine
and when do I stop?
How long do I dust the clumsy objects
formed by tender little hands?
Hands that are big and strong now.
Gone.
These things had a purpose once,
but now?
Am I the keeper of a museum?
It was agonizing to leave home.
Now it's hard to be back.
What is the answer?
Do you have a new role for me?
Lord, I am ready to move on.
Show me the way.
I don't want the ways of the past.
I've had enough of the old patterns.
My mind wants to expand.
My spirit wants to be free.

ð ð ð

I feel trapped.
Why am I frantic?
What's happening here?
Must I be alone to have peace of mind?
Why am I so easily over-powered?
Why do I take on responsibility
for someone else?
Will I ever learn when something is my fault
and when it is not?
Will I ever be at ease living with someone else?
Will I always take on his burden?
Am I still "loving too much"?
When does it end? Does it end?
Will I ever be free?
I want to be loving.
I want to be loved.
I don't want to be needed so much.
It's too heavy—I can't breathe.
Is it my fault?
I can't do the work for both of us.
Am I expecting too much?
Am I a mean person?
Am I back in the same trap?
What do I do now?

ta ta ta

Dear God,
The only thing I know for sure
is that I can trust You.
Even today's misunderstanding
is under Your control.
I know You send frustrations
when we're ready for our next lesson.
When we need another exercise
in what we think we've already learned.
It's frightening to try new ways.
Do I have it right?
What if I say too much—
will it be worse than before?
God, I can't turn back now,
but I'm so uncertain.
I'm trying to do what You taught me.
Why must progress be so hard?
Confrontations are horrible for me
because we don't seem to get anywhere.
Seems like we just silently agree to quit,
but nothing is changed.
Don't ever forsake me, God.
You are all I know for sure.

Words, words, words.
　Loving words,
　　gentle words,
　　　soft-spoken words,
　　seductive words,
　reassuring words,
intellectual words,
　rationalizing words,
　　elusive words,
　　　angry words,
　　sarcastic words,
　bitter words,
blaming words,
　apologetic words,
　　meaningless words,
　　empty words,
　　deceptive words,
　wasted words.
More words.

Words without action don't save a relationship.

ᏍᏍ ᏍᏍ ᏍᏍ

When you want your way
and I want my way,
we're in a power struggle.

When you manipulate to get your way,
even quietly,
and I give in to keep the peace,
we're in a power struggle.

When I think I'm right
and you give in sullenly
even when you don't want to,
we're in a power struggle.

When I blame you
for my unhappiness,
we're in a power struggle.

When I want something
and you won't give in,
and won't even discuss it,
we're in a power struggle.

When I tell my feelings
and you give me advice,
implying that I am wrong,
we're in a power struggle.

A power struggle might appear
to be about an issue that we disagree on.
But it's deeper than that.
It has to do with you and me,
how we are inside.
Our emotional health,
our past programming,
our protections,
our self worth, fears, inadequacies.
When we live in a climate of power struggle,
no one wins.
No matter who gets his way on a certain issue,
we both lose.
Everyone in the family loses.
There's something wrong.
We must find out what it is.

&a. &a. &a.

> 1   person sharing feelings
> + 1   person debating pragmatically
> = 2   persons in painful impasse

&a. &a. &a.

We must recognize parent-child interactions.
When you play the father,
and I'm the dependent little girl,
we need to change.
When you play the poor soul
and I'm the protective mother,
we need to change.
We're too old for these roles.
I lose respect for you and myself.
Our children might grow up before we do.
I don't want that.

ҙ ҙ ҙ

We are trying to communicate in a new way.
I hope we keep it up.
One person speaks—the other says what he heard,
and what it means to him.
What a difference there is!
We've been operating with different definitions.
We both speak English—at least we thought we did.
How can we have such a variation of word usage?
It's amazing to me that
two people who have become one flesh
can still speak in two languages.

ҙ ҙ ҙ

"I" messages are best.
I know how I feel.
You can only guess.
Most often when you tell me how I feel,
you are mistaken.
You may be projecting your own feelings
onto me,
putting my name on your feelings.
Please let me tell my own.
As I get a chance to tell my feelings,
that helps me—
I find out what they are.
When you tell me how I should feel,
that frustrates me
and often makes me angry.
I feel lectured to and I don't like it.
I don't want a diagnosis of my case.
I feel like you haven't understood at all.
Have you been listening?

≈ ≈ ≈

When my husband is mulling over something,
he looks sullen and withdrawn.
I think he's angry.
He looks like my father.
When I'm frustrated trying to explain something,
trying to sort it through,
trying to work it out,
I get agitated
and talk loudly and emphatically.
My husband thinks I'm angry.
Anger threatens him—it means loss of control.
That reminds him of his mother.
We are both learning
not to assume something about the other.
Instead we're learning that
when we are angry, we need to say clearly,
"I'm angry and this is the reason."
Or sometimes,
"I'm angry—
will you help me figure out the reason?"
I wish we'd known
how to do this
years ago.
I hope we master this lesson.

Dear God,
I'm calling out to You in anguish.
I hear judgments made against me.
"Why did she leave such a sweet man
when he worked hard
and gave her so much money?
He put all those children through college.
I thought she was a Christian."
My stomach knots.
The anger I thought was spent
consumes me in an instant.
I'm trembling—I begin to defend myself.
Why do I try? Why do I care?
Instinctively, I defend myself by blaming.
I hear my voice telling fragments of neglect,
hating myself all the while.
God, I don't want back in the blaming game.
I've fallen into my old trap of needing approval.
I thought I was healed.
God, how can I be so foolish?
I rehearse in my mind all that transpired
like I'm called before a jury and I'm pleading for mercy.
My husband and I are trying hard to begin anew.
We have a lifetime of programming to overcome.
We are both part of it.
Why do people try to judge who's at fault?
How can I fall into this same trap again?
The trap of justifying and wanting to be understood.

I am back to trying the impossible—
throwing the dolly in the ocean.
Dear God, thank you for You.
Forgive me for being so foolish.
If You are for me,
what does it matter that people are against me?
Help me to forgive them.
I can't do it without You.
I'm hurting so badly.
I'm remembering my mother—her litany of sorrow.
Oh God, don't let her be right
that we're always mistreated
and there's nothing we can do about it.
What is the worst thing that can happen?
It just happened—I let nameless insensitive voices
overpower the constant support You've given to me.
Underneath the lid of anger is my self-pity.
That's the worst—that's the pits.
I hate self-pity in others—I hate it in myself.
God forgive them, they know not what they do.
Forgive me too.
I can't change the ocean.
I can't change human nature.
But I can work through these setbacks much faster now.
God, thank you for helping me one more time.

ટ ટ ટ

It's hard to quit loving too much.
I need to join a support group.
I'm not a group person—I'm more comfortable alone.
Belonging to a support group
is like advertising something is wrong.
I've lived an image for so long,
it's hard to give it up.
Being a doctor's wife restricts my openness.
My husband is a very private person.
I don't want to embarrass him.
It's a conflict between his needs and mine.
Of course, that's the same old battle!
I can see how much I've withdrawn.
I'm trying to be honest with myself.
I had six good reasons to stay home,
but they probably weren't the real reasons at all.
How easily we fool ourselves.
There was security in isolation.
If a support group would help me,
I must try it.
I can't expect God to rescue me,
and then refuse to cooperate.
My husband is such a nice person,
it's easy for me to deny the problem.
I certainly did that long enough.
I didn't recognize our power struggle.
It was subtle, disguised.

I have to laugh when I remember
a salty old gal who lived in an apartment near mine.
"You keep saying your husband is a nice man.
If he's such a nice man,
why in the hell did you leave him?"
I had a hard time answering that one.
It doesn't make much sense, does it?
How easily I could slide backwards.
Denial brings immediate relief,
but it's only temporary.
I really do need to join
a group of women who love too much—
women who make the same mistakes I do.
They would understand me.
I dread going.
I suppose everyone is afraid
just like I am.
Everyone has fears of being truly known,
fears of admitting problems in public.

 za za za

To quit enabling is hard.
I must pray for the courage to do it.
I'm tempted every day to back down,
control, comfort, explain, give up my own plans,
go back to protecting and mothering.
God knows my struggle.
His support amazes me.
Seems like He answers me before I ask.
He guides me constantly, even in little things.
His presence is so important to me—
I would lose courage otherwise.
This is an uncertain time for me.
And yet, in some ways it is wonderful.
My confidence in God's voice has become
absolutely certain.
Knowing that God Himself
hears me and leads me
in my everyday life,
is a comfort beyond description.

&a. &a. &a.

When I tell you
my feelings,
and you don't hear me,
I wish I would stop telling them to you.

When I realize
that you don't want to understand,
maybe I will give up explaining.

Since you forget
what I say,
maybe I can stop caring.

If I ever get it through my head
that being closed to feelings
is a choice you make for yourself,
and you really don't want to change,
maybe I'll stop taking responsibility for us.
I won't feel guilty anymore.
I will begin to heal.
I will be free.
I will begin a whole new life.

&ps; &ps; &ps;

12 Another Move

I wake up to a strong impression.
"Go to Scandia." Another move?
I've become accustomed to God's guidance.
I'm tuned in to receive it.
When God has something for me to do,
He creates an intense desire within me.
It isn't a feeling of dread or obligation.
There's a special pull I recognize.
I won't barge ahead on my own.
If this is from God, He'll affirm it.
I go slowly—I'm encouraged along.
I've been to this place only once before.
Like before, an apartment is waiting
like it has been reserved for me.
I sense affirmation as soon as I see it.
A wooded haven of quiet beauty
where I can meditate, study, and write.
A sanctuary of sunlight.
A new life is ahead. I'm sure of it. I'm ready.
Maybe it's a retirement home for both of us.
It would be perfect—a whole new start
in a city where we could be equal.

ર૨ ર૨ ર૨

God has surely led me away again,
to this sanctuary in the woods.
I am more solid than before.
My faith is stronger.
I have self-confidence.
I learned many lessons last year
and there are more ahead.
God is the master teacher.
He will arrange my curriculum.
He understands how long I can struggle
before I need relief.
It's a pattern I've come to depend on.
I know from experience
how uniquely He ministers to me.
I cling to that knowledge when days are hard.
He knows what encourages me
and sends those very things:
words from someone dear to me,
moving music,
laughter from a child I love,
breezes, quietness, places to walk,
the flute-like song of a thrush.
Each one is given just when I need it—
signs of His presence chosen especially for me.
I am overwhelmed with gratitude.

❧ ❧ ❧

I've begun to go to Al-anon.

I like it. I fit in.

At Al-anon we don't need to hide our hurt.

We don't need to explain it either

because everyone already understands.

I don't need to have an alcoholic in my family.

I choose to go because I want help for myself.

Help for my own dysfunctional behavior.

That's enough reason for them to accept me,

and they do.

We learn how to live successfully

with a compulsive person.

A person driven to depend on a certain resource.

It can be work, alcohol, drugs, food, sports, whatever.

The emphasis is on myself.

I'm the only person I can control.

I cannot make choices for anyone else.

I cannot change another's attitude.

I cannot make him happy.

I cannot force him to grow.

Trusting God is encouraged—not ridiculed.

I like the people.

They are caring, upbeat, non-threatening.

They respect my privacy.

The program is consistent, reliable, proven.

I'm glad to be part of it.

⁂

God,
I'm having a hard time.
I spent thirty-five years trying to please my husband.
Being the one to hurt him is wrenching.
He doesn't understand my guidance from You.
I've tried to explain it so many times.
He hurried us to church every Sunday morning.
Why did we go?
It makes no sense to me to say formal prayers
and not expect an answer.
Why should we pray if we don't believe in guidance?
What good is it?
I know You are leading me.
I know I hear Your voice.
It's not audible,
but I hear it deep in my being.
This beautiful woods before me is proof—
it was Your voice that led me here.
I would never have come here on my own.
I'm really frustrated—
this has been an impasse for too many years.
How can I be happy
if he doesn't understand that I hear Your voice?
How can I follow You
if he doesn't understand Your command of my life?

෨ ෨ ෨

Dear God,
Is this the last time I'll see my dad?
He is frail.
Shaky.
His eyes are sunken and piercing.
It's hard for me to look at him.
What is he feeling inside?
I'm sad playing the game he taught me.
The game I continued in my marriage.
He set the rules for "Hide and Mask."
To avoid what is real with silly response.
To cover the ache with nonsense.
To spoof when we can't discuss.
To belittle because we're uncertain.
I don't think he knows
this is a game
where all the players
lose.
Is it too late?
Please, God, help me
not to teach this game
to anyone else.

≈ ≈ ≈

I'm taking a class in assertiveness training.
Why didn't I do this years ago!
We study communication,
how to say what we mean effectively.
I learn to speak
with courage without being aggressive.
Being assertive is not the same as being aggressive.
I use clear honest statements.
I do not hurt myself or you.
I have respect for myself and you.
We're both pleased with the result.
Being assertive is not manipulative.
Manipulation is sneaky,
a kind of sabotage.
I am learning to recognize verbal detours
designed to get me off track.
I'm learning how to defend myself against them.
I realize how often I've been taken in.
I learn to fight fair
without losing my self-respect.
I will inspire your respect for me.
I'll learn to say no without feeling guilty.
I'll take care of myself without mistreating you.
The class is fun and
I'm meeting new friends.

ða ða ða

Something very special is happening to me.
I am being healed.
God is healing me deep inside.
He has sent a special person to me.
But first let me tell you
about another person God sent to me years ago.

Her name was Mrs. Duff, a practical nurse who took
care of me after baby John died.
I was trying to be brave—that's all I knew.
I repeated to her the names of many of my friends,
and how sad they would be to hear the news.
They knew how badly I wanted baby John.
She listened patiently.
Sat beside me on the bed and gently asked,
"When are you going to let yourself be sad
because you know how badly you wanted baby John?"
Then she held me while I sobbed.
I have never forgotten her.

Now again, I'm trying to be brave.
I'm trusting God to direct my steps.
I know He led me away from home.
He made it clear to me and provided the way.
But I do not know His purpose,
and some do not hear His voice the way I do.
I grieve for them.

I've tried to explain my position
to ease their pain and also my own.
But I've given up—it's too hard a task.
The sorrow has remained
although my guilt is almost gone.
The burden's back on God—it's too heavy for me.

What is happening now is a marvel to me.
I cannot completely take it in.
So unexpected. So lovely.
An old friend has returned to my life.
A person I loved very much.
Our paths have crossed again
after thirty-five years.
What a welcome event!
What a wonderful surprise!
Only God could orchestrate such a joy.
He's not the same as when I saw him last.
Young, flippant, carefree.
Now he is worn, mellow, mature,
but his eyes still have their sparkle.
There is deeper expression in his face now
because he has experienced pain like I have.
How much we have to share—how easy it is to do.
I love him as before, only more.
Love is different for me now.
It doesn't have to be constrained
to a category or defined by a role.

I am free to love whoever God sends to me.
And He has sent my old friend back to me.
But even better than that,
He made friends with him first.
What a special treasure we share.
No one can take it from us.
It doesn't matter that each of us
belongs to someone else on courthouse records.
Our friendship transcends all that.
I'll tell you why.
This special friend has gently encouraged me
to tell my pain of years and years and years.
Of years before I knew him,
while I knew him, and since we parted ways.
It's easy because he already knows me so well.
I hold nothing back.
I am safe. I trust him.
I will not be misunderstood
because I know better now how to tell my story,
and he knows better how to listen.
But most of all,
God is with us, helping us
and healing me.
Healing both of us in unique ways.
Only He can do it.

ta ta ta

Dear God,
My suspense drags on.
I wonder what is next.
I remind myself that this is what faith is—
trusting You for what happens.
My life seems strange.
Waiting is the hard part.
Each minute has sixty seconds.
At night it seems like there are more.
How can I doubt Your control
when You have proven it so many times?
When the time comes, You work things out.
How soon will the time come?
What is going to happen to me?
You care for everyone—
You won't run slipshod over anyone.
How will You work this out?
I'm grateful I don't have to.
I only need to take one day at a time.
Sometimes one hour.
Sometimes, just this minute is a challenge.
Seems like I've been unsettled for a long time.
I miss a home—I'm a domestic person.
What is ahead for me?

﴿ﻠ ﴿ﻠ ﴿ﻠ

Oh God,
What is it?
What is this yearning?
This craving?
I need someone so badly.
I'm starving for someone.
Someone to be tender to me,
someone to have time for me,
someone to care.
Someone to care what happens to me.
I want to belong to someone.
I feel so small.
I feel so helpless.
I feel so scared—so shaking inside.
Is everyone like this or just me?
Why am I like this?
I'm aching for someone to love me—
to be kind to me—a safe place.
I've been strong for so long.
No, that's not true.
I've been pretending to be strong for so long.
Is that it, God—You want me to stop pretending?
You want me to admit
how frightened I feel inside?
If I admit how frail I feel inside,
maybe I will start taking care of myself
instead of everyone else.

Is that it, God?
Ever since I was little, I pretended I was strong,
pretended I was smart.
I couldn't admit how fearful I was,
how alone I felt
because I thought nobody cared.
It was too terrible to admit it—
to be stripped bare—
stand exposed, defenseless,
when no one cared.
I pretended to be strong,
and took on more and more and more.
Whenever I saw someone needy,
I understood their need and began to help them.
The more I helped others
the more needy I became myself
until now I finally see it.
I must quit this cycle—
this cycle of
   giving too much,
     depletion,
       yearning,
         pretending to be strong,
       giving too much again.
   Depletion.
I must admit my fear.
I must admit my emptiness.

How can I do it?

I can finally do it because of You, God.

You will surround me, protect me, comfort me, lead me.

I must admit my weakness

so You can give me Your strength.

I must quit giving strength to others that I don't have.

I must admit I don't have it.

I must ask for help from You, God.

I must practice until it is automatic.

Your strength will be made perfect in my weakness.

When I look to another person to be strong for me—

someone to lean on,

I am looking toward the wrong source.

I postpone the help You can give me.

When I pretend I am strong myself,

I prevent the help You can give me.

I have pretended for too long.

Starting right this minute,

I will admit my weakness—I will not pretend strength.

I will not try so hard—I will not reach so far.

I will not empty myself to depletion.

I will quit giving before I am depleted.

I will let You take care of me.

I will begin to take care of me.

When I learn to take care of me,

I will be strong without pretending.

ᕞ ᕞ ᕞ

My dad is gone.
He won't be at his desk anymore
updating his ledger.
It will take a while for my memories to settle.
The early ones—cherry picking days.
Later ones—through the words of my mother.
Pathetic ones of his grieving for her.
Happy memories of him talking with my children—
they still use his droll expressions.
Stressful times visiting him alone—
will he be mellow or caustic?
I have many gifts from him—an antique rocker,
an Amish quilt, my favorite paring knife.
When I admired it, he insisted I keep it.
I wish I could forget the ugly times.
In the nursing home, I know his belligerance
was a cover-up for fear and homesickness.
He snarled at me when I talked of God.
I wish I had handled it better.
He did not do well with abstract subjects;
he would retort with sarcasm.
I suppose he didn't know how to answer.
I wish I could hug him one more time.
He always smelled good.
I know he loved me.
I miss him today.

ია ია ია

Fragments of a scene years ago
come to the surface this morning.
A railroad platform in the dark.
A train roaring in.
How can I hug him goodbye
when I am angry with him?
My dad—
he was mean to mother.
That's what I told him my last evening home.
It was my last chance to help her.
I didn't go back for a year after that.
A long year.
I don't remember the issue exactly—
something about curtains.
Maybe he didn't help mother to hang them.
What did that have to do with me?
Nothing really, except the timing of it.
It happened after a summer of her sharing with me.
After three months of my absorbing her anger.
Anger too heavy for her to carry
so she unloaded it onto me.
It was too heavy for me,too,
so I hurled it at my dad—
my old buddy, who taught me to play pinochle.
Mother never knew the anguish she caused.
She never meant to—
she was not a malicious person.

She simply didn't know how to defend herself.
She was a product of her past.
A past I know nothing about
because she had it buried.
I know absolutely nothing
about her father or her mother.
Nothing. The record is blank.
It's too late to find out now—
everyone is gone.
I think that one burst of anger on her behalf
was so devastating to me,
I couldn't get angry with my own husband.
I would not take that risk again.
I tolerated anything
to keep the peace,
and protect my children
from an experience like mine.
I wish my high school had taught
family dynamics
instead of algebra and trigonometry.

ða ða ða

"I wish I didn't have to go,"
were my husband's parting words
whenever he left for work.
I believed him.
When he returned, he gave a message of tribulation—
an uncooperative patient, a badly behaved child,
a difficult delivery, an unnecessary house call.
I felt sorry for him. I needed to cheer him up.
He needed my support.
He needed me to manage things at home
to ease his heavy burden.
Whenever others remarked to me
that he was helpful, friendly, humorous,
I listened graciously.
I knew how hard he tried to please
no matter how tired he was.
I knew the price he paid.
I knew the price *we* paid.
The children and I asked for nothing
since he had already given so much to others.
I knew the real man.
The world saw the facade.
This drama went on for many years.
Now I wonder, who saw the real man?
Did he hate to go?
Did his negative message make it easier to leave?
Did he know that weariness was a message
I couldn't resist?

A signal I've responded to
since I was very small.
I gave myself to his worthy purpose
with unending loyalty.
I thought if I asked for nothing myself,
he would love me better.
Ah, that has a familiar ring to it!
I replaced a weary mother with a weary husband.
God knows how deep-seated my patterns are.
He knows we repeat the same ones.
Is this why He led me out?
Is this why He gives me unfailing affirmation?
He knows my loyalty.
He knows my sorrow.
He knows the guilt I carry.
He also knows my husband's role.
Did a message of weariness ease his guilt
for leaving me with such a heavy load?
Was it a pattern from his past?
Was it a manipulation?
If it was—I sure fell for it!
Will I ever know the truth?
Some days my grief is almost overwhelming.
He needs me and I'm not there.

ta ta ta

Dear God,
Thank you for this beautiful morning.
The ice encrusted trees are like crystal.
I love this sanctuary in the woods.
I delight in the birds singing.
Spring is coming soon.
I saw a robin yesterday in the midst of the storm.
How symbolic for me—
the sign of spring,
the promise of new life in the midst of my storm.
I have been violently uprooted
in the last few years.
Tossed back and forth like a tree in a storm.
My first apartment downtown—
the stark emptiness,
the shock of it,
the sudden expansion of my world.
And then the return home to my familiar kitchen.
I can picture it easily,
the morning sun coming across the counter top.
I timed my chores to use that morning sunshine.
But that is all past.
Now I'm in another city—another setting—
my lovely place in the woods.
The ravine, the river, the birds.
How I love it here.
Why, then, do I weep so much?

Does the beauty make me cry?
The closeness to You, God?
The reality of Your creation?
Early this morning the full moon
was shining through the silver trees.
All the while the redbirds were singing
and the woodpeckers were hammering.
So much energy manifested in the early dawn.
These are not tears of sorrow,
these are tears of awe
like the crystal on the trees.
How glad I am to have this quiet splendor
and the time to be immersed in it.
Why did You bring me here, God,
to this majestic beauty?
What are You planning for me?
Are You building me up for a special purpose?
Are You surrounding me with Your love
to prepare me for my next lesson?
An especially hard one?
Truly, this is the grace we hear about.
Amazing grace—undeserved love.
How grateful I am.
Small wonder I cry.
How foolish to ask what is next,
when the present is so magnificent.

ঌ ঌ ঌ

13 Highs and Lows of Divorce

Divorce is like a roller coaster ride.
Up one minute—down the next.
With dizzying speed,
I go from heights of exhilaration
to the depths of despair.
From the euphoria of new freedom,
I plunge into the pit of guilt.
My stomach feels hollow
as the bottom drops out of my life.
I feel out of control,
terrified that I'll fly into space.
Just when I'm going smooth and steady,
I'm thrust into violent rage.
Things come clearly into view one minute
to be gone again the next.
Sudden turns throw me off balance.
I hang on tight. Sometimes I scream.
In the suspense of an agonizing climb,
I wish I had never gotten on.
I can't wait till it's over.
Will this wild crazy ride ever stop?
Will I ever feel secure again?

ਃਨ ਃਨ ਃਨ

This is what happened—I'll tell it the best I can.
For a year I've lived in my sanctuary in the woods.
I've studied, prayed, and cried a lot.
Making new friends, rejoicing in old ones.
Waiting patiently. Waiting impatiently.
"Wait until May 15."
That's what I heard many times during meditation.
What was going to happen on this chosen day?
At last it came—a Sunday.
I went to church with my daughter-in-law
and my youngest son who lives with me now.
The sermon was on marriage!
My suspense was at fever pitch.
In the midst of his discourse,
the pastor paused, looked out, and said firmly,
"If one of these persons is not willing to change,
these vows don't deserve to be kept."
And that was it. My answer at last.
Here's the incredible part—it's hard to tell
because it sounds too bizarre.
When the official court document arrived,
it was stamped—June 6—a very special date in my life.
On that day twenty-five years ago,
God revealed Himself to me.
Three years ago, He began to reveal my life to me.
And now, what now?

&a. &a. &a.

Dear God,
The pain is awful.
All of a sudden a scene comes before me,
something from years ago.
Our canoe drifting on the quiet lake
in the evening stillness.
We shared the loveliness.
God, what happened?
How could we cherish that tranquility
and allow it to slip away?
Which is true—
the harmony I remember
or the shallow communication of today?
Both?
That's it—that's the answer.
Both are real.
Lovely times,
lonely times,
troubled times.
Impasse.
All part of the whole.
It is not simple.
The conflict is maddening.

ra ra ra

My conflict is maddening.
I go over the material—again.
Learn the same lessons.
Come to conclusions
I've come to before—feel the same relief.
I'm settled—this time it's permanent.
But it never is.
Will it ever be?
Will I wrestle with this anguish forever?
Is wanting freedom to grow such a crime?
Is making someone else happy my responsibility?
Is it possible to make anyone else happy?
It goes back to my basic addiction—
satisfying someone else
so my life has meaning.
Convincing someone else
so I know my case is valid.
Pleasing another
so I feel like a nice person.
Baloney.
I am a nice person.
Why can't I believe it?
I'm getting closer.

ᕗ ᕗ ᕗ

I'm not a bad person.
My husband is not a bad person.

We've both made some poor choices.
Poor choices can destroy a relationship.

Doing too much is a poor choice.
Choosing not to grow is a poor choice.
There are others.

It's never too late to change,
but it may be too late
to save a relationship.
Too late to save a marriage.

ൠ ൠ ൠ

Some mornings I wake up
hoping this whole thing was a bad dream.
To discover it's really happening
is a shock all over again.
How did it all begin?
God, give me another sign—
prove to me again that You're in control.

ൠ ൠ ൠ

I'm bogged down in confusion.
I read books describing dysfunctional families.
The case histories are clear cut.
My life isn't that obvious.
Can someone warm and loving
be passively punishing me?
I'm beginning to see
a dark thread running through my memories—
a somber link connecting isolated events.
Is this my imagination or
am I seeing what is true?
Silence, oversights, mistakes, tune-outs.
Subtle sabotage?
Quiet control?
I can hardly bear the thought,
but I can't stop thinking it.
Is it ever clear cut
what happens in a relationship?
Does it have to be someone's fault?
Seems to me that two products of dysfunction
merge to form another hurtful system.
I don't want to label our behavior good or bad.
I just want to be done with all this.
I'm sick of "who does what."

ta ta ta

I can try and try
to resolve differences with someone.
I can want very badly to end the turmoil.
It's not always possible.
When someone doesn't want to work on a problem,
there's nothing I can do.
When someone has built a wall around himself,
I can't get through it or break it down for him.
It must be cracked from the inside.
When that person is someone I love,
it makes no difference—the same rule applies.
It's difficult for me accept this fact,
a tremendous relief when I do.
When I realize it's no use,
I can quit trying to do the impossible.
I can begin to give up and move on.
Giving up can be progress—better than hopeless hoping.
The sooner I recognize I'm on the wrong track,
the sooner I get on the right one.
When at last I let go and allow someone
to suffer the consequences of his own choices,
maybe then he will begin to discover himself
and make some changes.
Maybe not.

੨ਅ ੨ਅ ੨ਅ

Is it possible
that some people
simply don't know
how to have a relationship?
They don't know there is such a thing.
They don't have a natural drawing toward other people.
Can this be?
I cannot imagine it,
but I believe I'm onto something.
It is not a matter of selfishness,
not rude thoughtlessness,
but merely a void of experience.
They simply haven't had experience
in caring and sharing.
Responding to others hasn't been important to them.
Reaching out doesn't occur to them.
They wouldn't know how to begin.
What is instinct for me is unfamiliar to them.
They don't have a feel for it.
Does past programming make some people
incapable of having personal relationships?
Do they even know they're missing something?
Can this be possible?

ta ta ta

I'm taking a divorce workshop at my church.
The leaders are skilled, dedicated, and caring.
Both men and women attend.
We're encouraged to share our pain.
I admire the self-honesty of the others
and their ability to be open.
Being a doctor's wife makes me hold back.
I'm still trying to protect my husband.
That's probably not the only reason.
Receiving attention for such personal material
is very uncomfortable for me, especially in a group.
How could I tell them God led me out?
They'd think I was out of my mind.
I don't want to reveal my hurting self.
I'm accustomed to being the helper.
I don't *belong* to a divorce group
because I don't *believe* I'm getting a divorce.
But, meanwhile, here I am.
Our vulnerability bonds us together
whether we are "dumpers" or "dumpees."
It makes no difference—we all have pain.
The intensity of divorce anger is explained to us.
We are prompted to vent our anger,
and taught constructive ways to manage it.
We learn that anger is necessary
to get the job done—we mustn't stifle it.
We air our bitterness, guilt, and self-pity.

We feel lonely, depressed, in shock.
Those with children have wrenching conflict.
We listen to each other with sincere concern.
One night the leader asked me,
"Do you ever allow yourself to cry?"
I replied jauntily,
"No, because if I did, I'd never stop."
She took the clue and questioned me further.
I proved my statement.
I sobbed uncontrollably for the rest of the session.
I heard her voice in the distance
firmly instucting me to take deep breaths.
The other leader held onto me.
It was horrible—and good
at the same time.
Does that make sense?
Needless to say, everyone was very kind to me.
Grief is normal—we have suffered tremendous loss.
Grieving our loss
does not mean we've made a bad decision.
We've lost our self-confidence.
We learn that divorce is a crazy time
that does eventually settle down.
We cheer our successes and begin to laugh again.
We move on with new hope.

ᘍᕐ ᘍᕐ ᘍᕐ

My ego was like a balloon.
Not a bouncy buoyant one,
but rather a deformed deflated
forgotten one.
Until—
God decided the time was right.
He lifted my squashed saggy self,
and started to fill me
with love.
His love
and love from His angels.
They thought they were my friends.
I knew they were God's angels.
They filled my ego balloon
so full—
now I can bob merrily about.
I don't need to worry about
sharp probes and piercings.
My covering is made of special stuff.
God's armor surrounds me.
When the day comes
that my earthly string is cut,
I will soar gracefully to heaven.
I know it.
I've been there a few times already.

ea ea ea

I hate to admit how bad I feel.
I feel like a child—
I want to sit on someone's lap and cry.
I want someone to hold and comfort me.
But, what if they give me advice,
lecture to me, and make me feel wrong—
I already feel wrong.
I like to think of myself as strong, confident,
sure of God's guidance, unwavering in my faith,
exuberant.
I am sometimes.
It hurts my pride that I'm not that way today.
I know that's foolish and unrealistic.
Feeling confused is human—we all get a turn at it.
It's not wrong—it's normal.
I hope I remember to allow others to fall apart.
I hope I don't give them pep talks and advice.
Today is my turn to be human.
I'm unable to love myself,
I'm disappointed in myself,
my pride is hurting.
I need love.
I won't always feel this bad,
but today I do.

❧ ❧ ❧

I don't want to waste any more time playing games.
They're not fun.
Here are some I've gotten caught in:
Pity me.
Be patient, look how hard I'm trying.
Why can't you accept me the way I am?
I need you—you help me more than anyone.
My happiness depends on you.
I can't do this without you.
It's all your fault.
You owe this to me.
Do it my way—I know how to punish you.
Keep dancing to my tune.
Keep waiting for me.
Sulk.
Sabotage.
Silent treatment.
You're crazy.
And many many others.
God, help me to recognize these tactics
sooner than I used to—
I'm not getting any younger.
Help me to play my cards better.
Help me to *quit playing.*

People look on my life of faith and
hear me tell about the inner voice I hear.
They hear the exciting parts,
the amazing answers and results.
They don't see me in anguish
struggling with conflict,
fighting doubt.
Is this direction from God
or am I making it up?
How can I be sure?
What if it doesn't turn out right?
I will look like a fool and
people will doubt the validity
of spiritual guidance.
That part is not my problem—
God can defend His own honor.
Has He ever let me down?
Even when things haven't turned out
the way I thought they would,
have they ever turned out really bad?
I've kept a record of prayers and answers
to support me in times like this.
How can I possibly doubt?
It's easy.

I dread opening "official" mail,
insurance forms, letters from my attorney,
financial matters, that type of thing.
I put off getting to them.
They intimidate me—
I'm threatened by legal language.
I dislike business procedures.
I know I'm not a stupid person.
I simply haven't had experience in these areas.
Now I must begin to learn.
I'll handle these lessons
as labor pains to my new life.
I'll tackle each challenge as it comes.
No one was born knowing all these things
and I can learn them too.
It's not too late. I'm not too old.
When I quit procrastinating,
I'll feel better about myself.
I will see life as an adventure.
I will be proud of what I've mastered.
I know I can do it
and I will.

ﺰ ﺰ ﺰ

Dear God,
How can he say I have a personality disorder?
He trusted me for thirty-five years.
He confided in me.
I raised his children successfully.
I handled his phone calls.
He reviewed puzzling cases with me
to get my insight and encouragement.
Now I have a personality disorder.
How much more humiliation can I take, Lord?
I guess it all fits in. I shouldn't be surprised.
You suffered the same experience.
It wasn't easy for You either, was it?
You did not defend yourself to the crowd.
I cannot defend myself to those who gossip.
Funny, it doesn't even hurt anymore.
I've had so much hurt, so much deep anguish
that I'm getting numb to public criticism.
Forgive them, they know not what they do.
Thank you for those who love me.
Thank you for those who are faithful to me.
Dear God, give each person who is suffering
at least one faithful friend or caring stranger.
Bring Your love to them through some divine channel.
Thank you for those You've brought to me.

&a &a &a

There was a promise
for the thief on the cross.
There was a second chance
for Simon Peter.
There was new insight and hope
for the woman at the well.
There was mercy
for the woman caught in adultery.
There was anger
for the haughty Pharisees.
I believe there is compassion
for those struggling with marriage vows.
I believe there is forgiveness
for those who part before death.

ða ða ða

Dear God,
Many times we pray:
"Thy will be done on earth
    as it is in heaven."
Then we continue to mumble:
"Deliver us from evil." [7]
Why are we so surprised
when You do it?

ða ða ða

14 And The Learning Goes On

What's my problem anyway?
My childhood wasn't so bad.
My parents weren't drunk.
They didn't even scream at me.
I wasn't abused. I wasn't molested.
I never went hungry. My basic needs were met.
Everyone around me was dependable.
What's the matter with me—
how did I get the way I am?

What about emotional nurturing?
Was I free to tell my feelings?
Was I listened to with respect?
Did I receive affirmation for my ideas?
Was I encouraged to trust others?
Was anyone aware of my needs?
Did anyone take time for me?
Did I feel enjoyed? Did I get hugs?
Did I feel loved? Did I feel wanted?
Was I dealt with honestly?
These answers are pretty clear to me.

How about the spiritual realm?
Jesus said "Man shall not live by bread alone." [8]

He said He was the way.
He came to give us abundant life.
Other than a few trips to Sunday school,
we had no spiritual emphasis.
We had no children's Bible story books.
God was not part of our everyday life.
There was no reference to God in conversation—
no prayer at mealtime.
On holidays when there was company,
we bowed our heads quietly for a minute.
What I remember best is
my dad's impish pinch under the table.

What about problem solving?
Did anyone reason with me logically?
Encourage me to face reality?
Did anyone suggest I work through a problem
to examine my part in it—probe some choices?
Demonstrate how to use anger effectively?
To be honest, I have some examples to give,
but I'm too embarrassed to share them.
I'm embarrassed just remembering them.
Let's just say that when parents are unsure of answers,
they don't invite questions.
When parents are uncomfortable with open discussion,
they discourage it in devious ways.
Inappropriate humor, sarcastic derogatory squelches.
Sometimes bizarre methods are used to avoid issues.

Deceptive means create confusion and distrust.
Guilt, shame, and rebellion take root.
Insecurity, low self-worth begin to grow.
I'm uncovering some significant data about myself.
Small wonder I don't trust my perceptions.

What about the social realm?
Was I proud of my home and family—or ashamed?
Was I encouraged to mingle with others?
Did I have a safe place of reassurance—
someone to turn to when I was threatened?
I might have to take a break from this study.
My stomach is churning.
I'm shaking inside.
I can hardly breathe.
I'm ready to start sobbing.
I'm in touch with a frightened lonely little girl.
I believe I've found some answers
to why I am the way I am.

Here are some facts I know for sure:
God loves me.
He knows my past.
He's helping me to work it through.
I'm making progress.

ॐ ॐ ॐ

There is seldom growth without pain.
The two go hand-in-hand.
Anguish is the coin of growth—
we must pay for progress.
When I avoid distress, I delay wisdom.
When I try to prevent someone's hurt,
I might be postponing their relief.
What a paradox—
my loving intervention may actually slow down healing.
Labor pains come before the joy of birth.
Likewise, struggle precedes fulfillment.
I'm beginning to estimate
the benefits of a lesson
by how much pain I have learning it.
My pain indicates transition.
Discomfort signals change.
Depression may be the hallmark of progress.
I no longer avoid it.
Good Friday came before Easter.
When we accept this fact,
thanking God for everything
begins to make more sense.

ᕒ ᕒ ᕒ

When I'm able to tell my feelings,
I have begun the process of discovery,
the process of growth, the process of healing.
Telling my feelings changes my behavior
    if I want to change my behavior.
When I work through my anger,
    I can explore the feelings underneath.
When I admit I feel guilty,
    I won't need to blame.
When I admit my self pity,
    I can start to work on the problem.
When I admit I feel helpless,
    I won't need to control.
When I admit I am hurting,
    I will begin to get relief.
When I admit my weaknesses,
    I can quit projecting them onto another.
When I admit my mistakes and ask for forgiveness,
    a new miracle has begun.
It has begun, but it won't be finished.
The process of discovery goes on forever.
I believe that if I want to grow,
God will lead me to each lesson I need.
He knows when I'm ready.

ᨒ ᨒ ᨒ

My counselor said I was "invisible."
I had not heard that term before.
I was like a shadow to those around me.
I did not maintain a solid form of my own.
Life was meaningful only as it related to others.
Easing another's life was my life.
I understand it better since I'm gaining substance.
A new word has gained popularity—
codependence.
If I am codependent,
I live my life through someone else.
It is different from cooperation.
It is the opposite of cooperation.
I am primarily a caretaker.
Sounds innocent enough,
but it can be a crippling disease.
Much is written now about codependence.
Help is available.
Having codependency recognized as a disease
is probably the biggest help of all.
Now that my self-defeating behavior is identified,
I can see it and work on it.
I can join others for mutual support.
To become visible,
I must first see myself.
I must learn to take my turn.

❧ ❧ ❧

Today I had some little visitors.
It was a long day.
Recent lessons became obvious
as I listened to them bicker.
How self-defeating to fret about someone else
instead of doing my own job.
Everything gets more complicated.
Simple plans take longer.
Angry words are spoken.
Feelings are hurt. Frustration abounds.
Most of all, the day is just not fun.
The dynamics of codependency
came into clear focus—a graphic picture.
I hated to watch how early this behavior begins.
No wonder it's so hard to change.

&a &a &a

When I continually help another,
I'm not doing a good thing.
It feels good in the beginning.
It's pleasant to be part of his life.
It adds meaning to my own.
Won't he be thoughtful of me in return?
Unfortunately, that's not always the case.
Why? What can be wrong? What causes the imbalance?
That's it—it's an imbalance. That's the key.

I do something. I do more. I do too much.
It becomes a habit. It becomes my lifestyle.
I don't stop to evaluate
whether my help is needed or wanted.
I'm still helping my mother.
I'm running the tape again hoping for a better ending.
When I give to others because I'm needy myself,
they get a locked-in feeling and resent my interference.
They might tolerate my behavior to appease me.
My help might be demeaning, unwelcome, and infuriating,
like my offer to the graduate nurse years ago.
And then there's another group to consider—
the ones who welcome my help.
Their lives are made easier through me.
They become accustomed to it—it's a good deal.
I could be in trouble.
I may attract some who take advantage of me.
I encourage a destructive exchange.
I cripple them. Spoil them.
I mislead them to think I don't have needs of my own.
I act like I'm strong, self-sufficient.
I deny myself the joy of receiving.
I haven't realized my part in this.
I want to quit this habitual caretaking.
I want people to enjoy me—not use me.

ﻫ ﻫ ﻫ

When God schedules a new lesson,
He plunges me into whatever I need to learn.
He puts it right in front of me
and lets me feel the discomfort.
He takes something from my past and
shows me my mistake.
If I have focused on romance,
He puts me in a romantic setting
and has everything go wrong.
He doesn't want it to fool me.
He doesn't want me to get caught in false substitutes.
False securities—
appearance, sophistication, respectability, prestige,
culture, affluence, whatever.
Cigarettes, alcohol, drugs, sex, food, anger—
the list goes on and on.
I truly believe that whatever I seek instead of God
to get relief from a need of the past,
a false security I have set up,
will be taken away or diminished somehow.
He wants me to delight in Him
first
and then
He will give me my heart's desire.
He will give me mature and healthy love.

&a &a &a

I have worshipped the god Education.
Even when I was small,
I sensed my parents were not educated.
I didn't blame them—they had no opportunity.
But it created a hunger within me.
I began my own push to learn.
Education would overcome whatever was wrong—
a kind of reliable cure-all—the answer to happiness.
I was relentless in my effort to improve.
Try harder. Learn more.
I believe that drive influenced my choice of a mate.
Only recently have I discovered that
education is not the answer to personal security
or satisfying relationships.
It doesn't eliminate fear or hurt.
Education is a valuable asset that enriches our experience,
and certainly improves the way we do some things.
But it is not an insurance policy for happiness.
It is definitely not a cure-all.
The first commandment puts it in proper perspective. [10]
We cannot make a god of knowledge.
It will disappoint us.
It will betray us.
Education is a false god.

&a &a &a

Pity is not the same as love.
Toward another or myself.
It is negative, restricting.
When I pity you,
I do not invite you to reach your full potential.
I keep you paralyzed in pathology.
When I feel sorry for myself,
that is the opposite of loving myself.
It is emotional cancer
that eats up healthy feelings.
Bad for me
and everyone around me.
My aversion to self-pity is so severe,
I react almost rudely.
One day I was tempted to put a sign on my door:
"If you've come here for pity,
you've come to the wrong place."
I didn't do it, but I better examine
why I react so strongly.
Has pitying someone
exacted a heavy price for me?
Do I hate self-pity
because I'm feeling sorry for myself
and don't want to admit it?

ਝ ਝ ਝ

People in dysfunctional relationships
have intense loyalty as well as denial.
My pastor tricked me into my first conference with him.
One day as I was speaking in jest,
this perceptive man heard my underlying message.
He recognized the pain cloaked in humor.
When he questioned me,
searing heat went all through me.
I was caught. The game was up.
God had scheduled my next lesson.
I poured out my heart.
Even so, when a second visit was suggested,
I responded in panic.
"I can't! It would be too disloyal."
I can't bear to disclose
that someone I love has let me down.
I don't want to make him look bad.
I'll feel too guilty afterwards.
I'm embarrassed—I'm well-known
and have projected a glossy image.
I'm afraid to risk the crutch I depend on—
the secure position of wife and mother.
I can't betray my strongest attachment.
And besides, it's not that bad.
Other people have it worse.
Maybe I'm expecting too much.

A pastor is busy with people
who have real problems.
He's late for his next appointment.
I don't want to stir up trouble.
It's better to leave it be.
I'll hang in there.
Wait a minute—that's an old tape!
It is not better to leave it be.
Examining a situation with a reliable helper
is not being disloyal.
It is honest and open.
It's a healthy step toward a better life.
But most of all,
God set me up for this.
He arranged it
because He sees my life better than I do.
My loyalty to Him overrides all others.
When He schedules something for my good,
I hold on tight and cooperate.

ʚ ʚ ʚ

Fear is an awesome thing.
It's power lies in my inability to recognize it.
Fear masks itself in a thousand ways.
How easily I am fooled.
A prized quality may be a cover-up for fear.
My docile nature may stem from fear of anger.
A tireless worker may be afraid of failure.
Hunger for learning may be the result of humiliation.
Financial success might spring from insecurity,
a fear of being dependent on another.
Social graciousness may hide a fear of disagreement.
The list can go on and on.
I may be afraid in my cozy living room,
threatened by ridicule, criticism, sarcasm.
Afraid of silence—I see it as rejection.
I fear a sigh if I suspect a hidden message.
I may fear a person close to me
and not even realize it.
I'm still discovering areas of fear in my life.
Some have motivated me to grow.
Some have caused paralysis,
keeping me locked in a certain response.
When I recognize a fear,
I'm on my way to freedom from it.
On my way to self-actualization.

&a &a &a

Going to a doctor threatens me.
Isn't that ridiculous?
I was married to a doctor and
my son is a doctor.
What is the basis of my fear?
I feel insecure in the modern bustling office.
"They don't have time for me."
Official forms confuse me.
Will I do it right?
"Color the square red and the circle orange."
Do I really have something wrong
or is it "all in my imagination?"
I doubt my perceptions. I don't trust my judgment.
I've lost my self-confidence.
Doctors are authority figures.
He knows more about my body than I do.
I feel self-conscious and embarrassed.
Will I tell my story so it makes sense?
Am I still "wet behind the ears?"
Will I be listened to with respect?
Will the doctor think my complaint is trivial?
Will he ridicule me to his colleagues?
What is all this?
Old scars are screaming out.
Old tapes are playing at top volume.
What can I do? That's the good news!
There are many things I have learned to do.

First, I recognize what is happening.
I am kind to this child—me.
I have learned by experience what is helpful.
I must detach if possible to sort things through.
Sometimes a time-out in the rest room is enough.
Gives me a chance to calm down,
ask myself questions.
Check what's happening *underneath* what's happening.
Gives me a chance to talk to God—He won't laugh at me.
Remember this is a process.
A process of dealing with reality.
Separating the past from the present.
What's really happening? What choices do I have?
I must ask questions if I need help.
Keep trying.
Meet the challenge in front of me.
There's a powerful dynamic going on. It's valid.
I'm not the only one this happens to.
It's not as silly as it seems.
It's a chance to heal old wounds.
God's process of healing.
I thank Him for each experience.
I remind myself that "all things
work together for good for those who love God." [9]
God is the Healer who does not threaten me.

&. &. &.

Love and addiction—what is the difference?
Love is healthy,
    expanding,
        productive,
            fulfilling,
                freeing.
Adult love means individuality with mutual caring,
giving and receiving, celebration. Separateness.

Addiction is self-defeating,
    narrowing,
        destructive,
            never satisfying,
                killing.
Addiction is an overpowering need for love.
It is the opposite of love.
It grows from a seed of fear and emptiness.
Relationship addiction means possessive yearning,
waiting, disappointment, anguish. Enmeshment.

When I'm able to love myself,
I reach out from a strong center
to those around me.
I am a blessing to myself and others.
My source of love is God.

                      🙚 🙚 🙚

I want to learn more about addiction.
I know it stems from feelings of
helplessness, emptiness, fear.
I need something to relieve my feelings.
I need a source of comfort, strength, or escape.
It can be a substance, activity, or another person—
whatever works to relieve my anxiety,
fill my void, empower me, comfort my yearning.
Maybe I can examine addiction
by reviewing my own story.
I'm a lonely little girl waiting for attention.
I long for it.
I develop a dream—someday I will belong to someone.
Someone will fill my emptiness.
    Someone will be there for me.
    Someone will care what happens to me.
    I'll pay him back with my devotion and understanding.
    I will have a purpose—I will be needed.
    I'll stand behind him as he faces the world.
    We will be a world unto ourselves.
Dreaming becomes
an escape of increasing dosage and frequency.
I begin dating at an early age.
I smile and look pretty—my date takes care of me.
As my personality evolves,
I require a more commanding figure;
but the pattern remains the same.
I lean on someone older, educated, more socially at ease.

I fit into his plans, asking nothing for myself,
expanding my world through his world.
He is my resource for safety and fulfillment.
My fantasy escape becomes reality.
While it might appear on the surface
that my attachment to a stronger person nourishes me,
that is not the case.
An underlying process diminishes me.
My inner child of the past merges with that person
in a familiar system. I walk a worn path.
I actually reproduce my old system.
I strive to please and invite neglect.
My need to be attached dominates my life.
An addictive bond is established.
Its hold on me takes root like
a cancer that will erode my strength.
An octopus that will strangle my freedom
and choke my development.
There's another aspect to this connection—
a person accepting such an imbalanced partner
is very likely to be out of balance too.
A healthy mature person would not enjoy
my clinging relationship.
He would feel stifled by it.
He would be wary of my dependence—
not flattered by it.
My judgment skills are so immature,
appearance and manner fool me.

They camouflage underlying traits.
Strength in one area masks weakness in another.
My need for attachment makes me excuse
and ignore any warnings of disadvantage.
I lean on a strong silent type
without admitting he is dull or insensitive.
I feel at ease with a warm attentive person
and deny that he is irresponsible.
I am secure with a steady dominant figure
not realizing he is controlling and possessive.
I am attracted to one quality,
and torpedoed by another.
There are damaging side effects to addiction—
even people addiction.
My need for attachment is so great,
I don't make wise evaluations.
As I look back, my dysfunction becomes clear to me.
I can trace it through all my relationships.
I recognize my intense need.
I'm aware of the strangle hold of addiction.
To break loose is a herculean task.

ﻙ ﻙ ﻙ

I am compelled to keep studying.
I learn how two needy persons fit together—
their bond intensifying in mutual addiction.
Their union hollows out a deepening rut of isolation—
a stricture of experience and expression.
The world doesn't see the consuming dysfunction.
The individuals themselves might not be aware of it
until—one member begins to grow.
One wants to reach out for new things,
broaden experience, become whole.
Become a whole, not just a half.
When one person in a relationship wants to be whole
and the other wants to remain a half,
there is conflict.
Confusion. Anger. Guilt.
When one wants mature love instead of codependence,
power struggles are inevitable.
Misunderstanding abounds.
Withdrawal symptoms create terror.
Separateness feels like rejection.
The old addictive system is dying,
but it is not a sudden death.
It's a transition of agonizing torment.
A process of emotional turmoil
that may go on for years
until we finally break loose
from this pathologic system.

I am fascinated by addiction
because I've been struggling toward wholeness
for four years.
I'm almost there.
It is wonderful!
I'm glad I didn't give up.
I'm glad I didn't give in
to those who didn't understand.
To those who wanted me to stay
in a system we didn't know about.
I heard God's voice.
He heard mine.
He understood my situation—I did not.
He led me forth.
He is leading me out of my personal addiction.
I believe He wants me to tell my story.

ع. ع. ع.

A whole family can operate under an addictive system.
When we're overly involved with each other,
when separateness is lacking,
addiction can be suspected. We are enmeshed.
We haven't developed healthy autonomy.
As a parent, I can be addicted to my children—
unable to let go.
I hang on instead of giving them encouragement
for growth and independence.
This is the opposite of healthy love.
If I'm a smothering controlling parent,
I am filling a need of my own.
My ego structure needs support.
I'm filling a void.
Children need freedom to make their own choices.
They need a chance to make their own mistakes.
Healthy struggle promotes expansion.
Individual growth builds resistance against addiction.
Oh God, help me to encourage their independence.
Help me to let them go
for their own good as well as mine.
Help me to have tough love.

ঌ ঌ ঌ

This whole idea of codependence
is beginning to make sense to me.
Codependents attach to compulsive people.
We are trained to adapt.
Compulsive people are out of balance.
They have an extreme level of intensity.
They require activity
like alcoholics need a drink.
They have difficulty establishing limits—
do very few things in moderation.
They go from one activity to another
in rapid succession with incredible absorption.
Whoever could fit in with such frenzy?
Who could endure it?
Who would choose to be part of it?
Aha!
Who thrive on others like parasites on a host?
Codependents, of course.

ta ta ta

A compulsive person with a quick sense of humor
is great fun
for a short time.
A longer period can get destructive for me.
I can't keep up. I feel dull and slow.
I am embarrassed.
I want to escape and be alone.
When humor becomes an arena of competition—
one-upmanship,
I don't enjoy it.
I feel overpowered and defeated.
I want to slink away.
I feel small and sad.
I'm beginning to learn I don't need to compete.
I can choose to simply laugh and enjoy the others.
I don't need to join in.
Sometimes the banter gets just plain boring
and I choose to do something else.

 за за за

"We tease you 'cause we love you."
How often have I heard that!
In fact, I've said it myself.
I'm not sure I believe it anymore.
When I'm teased, especially in front of others,
I don't feel loved—I feel betrayed.
I'm at a disadvantage. Embarrassed.
I can't think of a reply—repartee is not my style.
To show anger makes it worse.
I turn from poor soul to poor sport.
But I feel angry inside.
My swallowed anger turns into resentment and mistrust.
I don't feel loved—that's for sure!
Maybe teasing is a juvenile form of control
when the teaser feels uneasy himself.
Maybe a sneaky form of revenge.
It might just be family fun and personality
passed on from one generation to the next.
I admit, it's fun when it's just you and me.
Then it doesn't get out of hand.
I guess the main thing is timing
and knowing when to quit.
Of course, it's the most fun
when I've got something on you!

ᴥ ᴥ ᴥ

I got a letter "from my husband" today.
I wrote it myself—a great idea!
I said all the things I've wanted to hear.
It was an exhilarating experience.
I wrote pages and pages and pages.
I might add more.
A unique way to finish unfinished feelings.
He's sorry he caused me so much pain.
He didn't realize what my needs were.
He wishes our communication had been better.
He's sorry he didn't hear what I said
and what I didn't say.
He didn't know how forsaken I felt,
how badly I wanted our marriage to be special.
He didn't realize how hard it was for me
to be stranded, so young,
in a place familiar to him—strange to me.
Waiting, waiting, waiting. Hoping.
He didn't realize how exhausted I was
being mother and father.
He appreciates the respect I taught the children.
He doesn't take it for granted anymore.
He understands my grief.
He forgives me for leaving him.
He cries too.

ૐ ૐ ૐ

We follow childhood patterns—
even those we hate.
It is ironic and tragic.
Grown up victims produce more victims.
The patterns repeat over and over.
"The sins of the fathers
rest upon the children for generations." [10]
A helpless child, afraid of his father,
becomes a controlling tyrant
when it's his turn to father.
A child of dysfunction propagates dysfunction.
Is there no end?
Is there no hope?
I believe there is.
With God all things are possible.
Through God there is help,
    forgiveness,
        healing,
            a new chance.
Through God miracles happen.
Breaking the chain of dysfunction
is nothing less than
a miracle.
I believe miracles still happen.
I believe one is happening to me.

❧ ❧ ❧

There's a cemetery where I walk.
It's more fitting than strange
since I'm mourning the death of my marriage
as well as the loss of old familiar patterns.
I love it there—I walk undisturbed.
I talk out loud to God as I walk.
Curving paved roads
let me walk in any weather.
It's safe for me to go there alone
to enjoy early morning freshness
or the splendor of sunset.
I can embrace a vast expanse of clear sky
or trudge along in mist and drizzle.
I watch seasons record on the trees—
my favorite is a giant oak outstretched beside a pond.
Brilliant now,
they will soon be bare for the winter's rest.
When they burst forth again in the spring,
I will rejoice with them
because I know we're all together in God's plan.
God loves me along with them.
My life has seasons too.
Each one has value and definite purpose.
I think He has a new life ahead for me—
a time when I will burst forth into full blossom.

ta ta ta

15 New Patterns At Last

When I look back I see clearly
    how small my child world was, how sheltered.
I see how young I was when I got married,
    how hard I tried with the knowledge I had.
Always hoping. Always dreaming.
There were good times—
    they kept me hoping, dreaming, trying harder.
Some of it is a blur—
    headaches, weariness, phone ringing,
        six children at the table.
It's mind-boggling to think
    how much I must have cooked,
        how many clothes I put into the washer.
Being a mother was easy for me though—
    it was all I ever wanted.
I gave it everything I had.
I would be there yet if God had not stepped in
    to interrupt the pattern—
        to lead me to a bigger world.
I was losing myself. Becoming invisible.
My life was meeting needs of other people.
Putting them first—their life was my life.
I thought that was unselfish love.
In truth it was relationship addiction.

Focusing on someone else eased my emptiness.
When I helped, I felt wanted. I belonged.
There was meaning to my life.
I thought it was good for those around me.
God showed me my mistake.
I'm breaking from that lifestyle
to "do my own thing."
But, what is it? What is *my thing?*
What is my purpose—how will my life have meaning?
What will I do with my time?
How will I expand myself? Where do I start?
What are my choices?
Now that I have my turn—what do I do with it?

ta ta ta

"Doris is full of the Gochenauer."
My mother's pronouncement—not complimentary.
Her mother-in-law's maiden name was Gochenauer.
As I heard it, she meant my independent spirit.
I got angry sometimes. I was not a nice girl.
Nobody would like me. Shame on me.
I bet a lot of healthy behavior was under that label.
From now on I won't shrink from it.
I'll rejoice in it. Viva the Gochenauer!

ta ta ta

How do I start?

With a list of things I'm thankful for.

No special order. It's just for me.

A way to gear up for my new life—a new healthy life.

I'm thankful I can choose to be happy in it.

I can choose my attitude—God has given me that choice.

That's no small thing—it's powerful!

I'm thankful I can choose my attitude.

I'm thankful for my physical health. I can walk.

For my eyes—I can see the faces that I love.

I can see this beautiful woods and sparkling river.

I'm thankful for my apartment—

it's warm on this cold windy day.

I'm thankful for the sunshine pouring in.

I always yearned for sunshine in my living room,

and now I have it. I delight in it.

I'm thankful for the telephone.

I'm thankful I have people who call me.

I'm thankful for my new answering machine.

It feels good to come home to the blinking signal.

I'm thankful I have food for my body,

and books—food for my mind and spirit.

I'm thankful for good things and bad things

because I don't always know the difference.

I'm thankful that God does. I'm thankful for God.

ᘗ ᘗ ᘗ

I'm thankful for God.
What an understatement that is.
I can't imagine coping in this world
without God's help.
Sometimes I think people don't understand
how much power is really there,
and what a difference it can make.
Otherwise, they would latch on.
Seems self-defeating not to. What a puzzlement.
Maybe it's because of bad examples from the past.
I believe the key in the present is spiritual food.
Spiritual food is like other food—
I need some every day.
When I pray, I talk to God.
When I read His Word—He talks to me.
He feeds me.
Food is digested so I have strength to live.
God's word is absorbed for the same reason.
His spirit infiltrates me to empower my responses.
But a God-centered life is much more than that.
There's *power* there. Real intervening power.
Help when I need it. Direction.
I do my part—daily food and prayer.
God does His part—His part is beyond description.
His part is incredible.

ᐤ ᐤ ᐤ

For years I've kept a notebook—
an assortment of things—
favorite passages from many sources.
Nuggets that helped me along the way.
My collection is titled
"Instant Salt—for when I lose my flavor."
A kind of first-aid kit for emotional emergencies.
When I'm sad, when life deals me a hard time,
when I get off track,
when I'm beginning to lose my flavor,
I turn to my book of instant salt.
Help comes in a few minutes.
Proven passages boost my sagging spirit.
Having it readily available is a big help
when I feel too dreary to search anew.
I don't flounder aimlessly
wasting my own time,
and dragging down those around me.
My thankful list will be part of this supply.
I will keep adding to it.

ಕ ಕ ಕ

When I was first learning to depend on God,
I used an easy and practical method.
The phrase, "I'll put it in my book"
was familiar to my children years ago.
It meant a business-like transaction
with a God who was reliable for me.
I need to get back to it again.
I record what I turn over to God—
problems, sorrows, questions.
I leave a space to fill in the answer.
My doubts and anxieties are dispelled
through this consistent method.
My spiritual life shifts from vague feeling
to a system of orderly procedure.
When my faith is at low ebb,
I review the uncertainties of the past
and the certainty of the answers—
God is faithful.
He's more faithful to me than I am to Him.
He continued to answer my needs
even when I forgot to enter them.
This register is more for me than God.
He doesn't need reminders of His reality—I do.
Entries of confidence and trust
in my safe deposit book.

ða ða ða

When I was first led away from home,
I devised a scheme.
I needed a plan to spur me to grow and expand.
A kind of game I played.
Each day I had a challenge:
I had to do one new thing,
talk to one new person,
or go to a place where I hadn't been before.
I took a new risk.
Before I went to bed at night,
I wrote the day's attempt on my calendar.
It felt good to meet my goal.
It gave me a sense of accomplishment
that's important in times of depression.
My scheme was successful—I did grow and expand.
And I did face reality.
I'll be grateful forever.
I don't need a regimented plan of attack anymore.
Doing new things is easier for me now.
I venture out spontaneously.
There are opportunities all around.
It's a wonderful new way of life.

&a &a &a

I have a new job
in a fashionable clothing shop.
It's an ideal way for me
to work with lingering insecurities
from my inner child of the past.
I will learn procedures unfamiliar to me.
I'll relate to others in a new way.
I already share easily with people who are hurting.
Now I'm going to learn to exchange pleasantries
with breezy, confident people.
Become resilient to those who are rude—
develop a "thicker skin."
It's all part of a balanced life.
I'm going to pay attention to styles.
Learn about coordinating colors.
Ask questions about accessories.
I won't be too shy or too proud
to admit what I don't know.
When I gain more expertise,
I won't feel awkward and homespun anymore.
I'll be glad to give up that image of myself.
When I master this challenge,
I'll try something new.

ᏋᎧ ᏋᎧ ᏋᎧ

I'm beginning to travel.
Alone—but not alone.
My support system goes with me.
I'm not lonely.
There's a special blessing in this solitude.
As I drive along this winding way
of blooming dogwood and rippling streams,
a familiar psalm sings in my heart. [11]
I have my own words:
"The Lord is my best friend,
my needs will be met.
He created me to enjoy the beauty of His earth.
He leads me to glistening waters.
He restores my soul.
He guides me to obey Him in His honor.
Yea, tho I walk again through pain and confusion,
I will not fear
for You are with me.
Your Word and Your Voice—they comfort me.
You send help in the depths of my sorrow.
You pour love on my wounded spirit
until my joy is overwhelming.
Surely, there will be no end to this glory
because I have found it to be real."

&a. &a. &a.

I can make choices.
I can choose what is good for me.
That might not sound like much,
but to a woman who has loved too much,
and given in too easily,
it is a powerful feeling. Exhilarating.
First I evaluate what is happening.
Then I thank God for the situation.
I identify my feelings and—here's the big part—
I choose what I do!
It may be exhilarating, but it won't be easy.
I'll fall back into old patterns sometimes.
Almost every minute is a chance to practice.
What is happening? I thank God for it.
How do I feel? What do I choose to do?
I want these four steps to become automatic
so I'm ready for sudden situations.
What happens to me is not as important as
how I handle it—what choice I make.
Even waiting for a phone call has options.
I'm going to make a game of this.
It's my move. It's my turn!
Relationships will change
when I respond differently.
I'm alive with anticipation—my life is new.

ം ം ം

I expect to have bad days once in awhile.
Days when I feel empty with no real purpose.
I want to have a home and belong to someone.
Sometimes I ache to belong to someone.
I get homesick for my husband.
I want to call him
like an alcoholic wants a drink.
I call to God instead.
I admit I feel terrible—I'm out of control.
I have the "codependent crazies."
I'm not surprised. I expect relapse.
I am kind and patient with myself.
I remember God is in charge
because I've asked Him to be.
I talk to Him openly like He's a friend in the room
or riding in the car with me.
I feed on Him.
I read my salt book, the Bible, or other helpful material.
I ask God to lead me to what I need.
It is truly amazing what appears.
A passage touches me in a dynamic way.
An impact of certainty.
If we believe the Bible is God's word,
why wouldn't He use it to speak to us
specifically for the subject we're asking about?
It's that simple.
It's my job to believe it,
depend on it for each day's challenge.

I can't keep talking to Him
without giving Him a chance to answer—
that's just plain bad manners.
This morning I "just happened upon"
"Depend on the Lord in whatever you do.
Then your plans will succeed." [12]
It was exactly what I needed to hear.
Depression is a good time for learning—I am open.
I write down my feelings.
I don't try to escape from them.
Sometimes I hold on to something soft.
A pillow, a pet, a stuffed toy, a real baby.
I set a small goal.
The dishes need to be washed. I do them.
I thank God for the chair I'm sitting in,
the clothes I'm wearing, move outward from there.
I take a walk outside.
I knit or sew. I don't watch T.V.
I don't want to waste this chance to grow.
I call a friend who understands codependence.
One who knows I need affirmation.
When I am depressed my self-esteem drops.
I avoid people who are quick to give advice.
Unwanted advice is demeaning.
If I haven't reached the real problem,
their hasty advice is meaningless and irritating.
I want to keep my self-respect.

I want to work out my own problem—it takes time.
I review my progress.
I know some good things about me.
I remind myself of the people who love me.
Sometimes I actually write down their names.
I wait. I trust. I begin to feel better.
I repeat the doses of comfort, prayer, reading,
learning, setting goals, exercise, and affirmation.
This attack will pass.
I will have new energy. New expectations.
Life will have meaning again.
I know it. I have tested it. I am sure of it.

&a. &a. &a.

It's okay for me to grieve.
Even though I have new patterns,
I've lost my old ones—unbalanced as they were.
The wilderness wanderers yearned for Egypt
where they were slaves!
It's natural to mourn losses.
I have a new life, but I've lost my old one.
I have new joy, but I still have unspent sorrow.
I can have both at once. It's not a contradiction.
It's not surprising.

&a. &a. &a.

Do you want to know how to love me?
Do you really want to know?
Because I finally have the answer.
Here's how I feel loved—it's pretty simple.
When I'm excited about something,
listen to me.
When I have just learned something
that reveals me to myself
and I want to reveal me to you,
better than before,
listen to me.
When I have new understanding of life,
and I want to celebrate it with you,
listen to me!
When I have joy, laugh with me.
When I have anxiety
and I need to uncover the reason,
please listen to me—
it's not usually what comes out first.
The source of my fear is often deep inside—
a carry-over from the past.
When you listen to me with genuine respect,
I won't be fooled. I'll sense your caring.
I'll feel loved and very grateful.
Life will feel good to me again.

ご ご ご

Finding good listeners takes a long time.
In the past I was so hungry to be heard,
I didn't choose listeners carefully.
Often they were ignorant of listening skills
like I was.
I was so needy and inexperienced,
I didn't know where to find a wise person.
I set myself up for frustration and embarrassment.
Good listeners don't say much.
They convey gentle awareness.
Depressed people need affirmation—not advice.
Giving advice to someone who needs comfort
adds resentment and more hurt.
When we are down we feel inferior.
Advice makes us feel even worse.
I discover once again
that hard lessons have great rewards.
My present family of listeners makes my life rich.
They truly hear me, and besides that,
they have taught me how to listen.
We share a bond beyond words.
A bond of perceptive caring.
I am truly blessed.

ੇ੨ ੇ੨ ੇ੨

A basic truth has come alive for me
offering welcome relief from much frustration.
Here's the pearl—
if a person can't be honest with himself,
he can't be honest with me. That's it.
If he can't be honest with me,
what good is our communication?
If our communication is not reliable,
what have we got?
If I accept what is presented as trustworthy
when it isn't, I am led into a maze of confusion.
I can stumble in circles a long time
until I reach truth—
this person is not being honest
with himself or me. But why?
Maybe he is afraid.
Afraid of feelings he can't handle.
Maybe that's why he protects himself
with rationalizations, contradictions,
and memory lapses.
One thing is certain—
anyone who is not honest with himself cannot grow.
Honesty is necessary for emotional and spiritual growth.
Mutual honesty and growth
is necessary in rewarding relationships.
It's futile for me to keep trying
to share growth and understanding with someone
who doesn't want to find new answers.

Answers that might reveal
what he's afraid to experience.
If someone is afraid of truth,
he can use any number of protections—
denial, silent treatment, detours, blaming,
abuse, addictions, whatever works.
I can't get through a protective wall.
I'm going to give up the impossible.
End futile expectations and disappointment.
I'm too old to keep "throwing a dolly in the ocean."
I've had enough of this self-defeating quandary.
Who needs it?
I gladly give up a lot of grieving and guilt.
I want emotional health and realistic problem solving.
I want spiritual fellowship.
I want dependable adult relationships.
I enjoy quality communication.
I recognize the difference.
I'm really excited about it.

ᴥ ᴥ ᴥ

The old Doris was a professional "happy-maker."
I should have hung out a shingle
like shoe-repair or alterations.
I could have advertised in the yellow pages:
"Come to me if you are
weary, frustrated or frazzled.
I will take time for you.
I will try to help you.
I will share my zest for living.
In business since 1935.
Satisfaction guaranteed."
Now I have a new improved system.
I offer the same basic service—the same caring,
the same enthusiasm—with one notable difference.
Now you must qualify—you must want to get better.
You must be willing to change.
You must make an effort on your own behalf.
Because if you don't,
I am not obligated to give you any more of myself.
I'm not responsible for your happiness.
I will not feel guilty.
I won't "throw my pearls before swine." [13]
Before Jesus healed the lame man, He asked him:
"Do you want to get well?" [14]
I ask the same.

ða ða ða

Sharing is different from dumping.
One is the means to an end;
the other is an end in itself.
As you talk to me, I can sense your intent.
If you're airing your ideas for further study,
I can recognize your effort.
Your voice has a positive tone.
You are questioning and examining,
working for progress.
I like progress—I like to be part of yours.
It helps me to learn.
It's invigorating and feels good.

When you are dumping on me,
it feels just like that—
like you are dumping a load on me.
It's unpleasant, dragging, heavy.
When you repeat complaints that I've heard before,
I almost know what's coming next.
I brace myself for your excuses.
I resent giving up my time.
I feel trapped.
Allowing you to continue dumping on me
doesn't do either one of us a favor,
and I won't cooperate anymore.

ʒ₳ ʒ₳ ʒ₳

Cooperation is different from codependence.
When we have cooperation,
we are both productive.
We are both growing.
We both want to be responsible for ourselves.
We share ideas.
We give encouragement.
We give support, but we take turns.
We each receive.
We are equal.
We respect each other.
I want to cooperate with you;
I don't want to be codependent.
I want to share your load,
but not pull it for you.
I'm glad when you carry your own.
I'm enriched by our sharing,
but not dependent upon it.
I am healthy.
I am free.
I like you.
I like me.

ک ک ک

I'm angry—yes I am—I am truly angry.
And I hate it.
I'm angry with myself and someone I love.
For me to admit I'm angry with someone I love,
and plan to do something about it
is front page news.
It takes all the courage I have.
I've just run the vacuum cleaner
to work off my frustration.
Sometimes I pound my bed.
Yes I do. I get down on my knees,
and pound as hard as I can.
The people in the next apartment can't even hear me.
I feel foolish, but I do it anyway,
because it helps me to vent my fury.
The fury that I'm finally allowing myself to have.
Some people jog. Some scream. I pound.
Today running the sweeper is enough.
I've figured out why I'm so mad.
I've written it down.
And now—
I'm going to tell that person
how angry I am
and why.
I won't have to scream and lose control,
because I've just pushed and shoved the vacuum cleaner.
I'll need to think clearly
to stay on the subject—I hope I can.

Under my lid of anger is fear.
What's the worst that can happen? That's easy.
The worst thing would be to lose the person I love.
Would I really—what are the chances?
If defending myself and expecting better treatment
makes me lose the person I love, maybe it's no loss.
Why would I want to continue
a relationship with someone who mistreats me?
What kind of love is that?
So what do I do?
I've already thanked God for what has happened.
I thank Him that all of this can be used for good.
I know the biggest lessons hurt the most.
I've gotten in touch with exactly what happened.
What was done to me and why it hurt.
How many times it has happened before.
I see how I've contributed to the problem.
I'm going to work on my part.
Now I'm ready to state my case—
because I do have a case.
I've been treated unfairly—it's not in my imagination.
I have good reason to be hurt.
I know what that reason is.
I want him to understand how he hurt me
because I respect myself.
I'll find out how he responds.
I'll listen carefully to what he says,
and pay attention to what he does.

Will he listen or tune me out?
Will he gloss over or discuss it reasonably?
Will he say he's sorry and make the same mistake again?
Will he be truly sorry and make an effort to work on it?
My anxiety builds. I hate confrontation.
One thing I know for sure—it is not wrong to be angry.
It's not wrong to be hurt or disappointed.
It is human. It is healthy!
It is wrong to let the same thing happen repeatedly.
It's wrong to deny the problem
for fear of losing him or his love.
It is wrong for me to take all the responsibility
because I'm willing to work on a solution.
It's wrong to make excuses for him.
It's wrong for me to use someone else as a scapegoat.
I used to take my anger out on my children
because it was safe—I was sure of their love.
I wish I hadn't done that. I feel bad about it now.
I'm glad I finally know a better way.
When this settles down, I'll evaluate how it works out.
If I'm satisfied, I'll drop it and forget it.
If not, I'll process further
in a logical, healthy way.
I'll take care of myself—
a daring new adventure!

᠁ ᠁ ᠁

People from dysfunctional families have secrets.
Things we are ashamed of—things we hate to admit.
We carry them around subconsciously.
We hold them prisoner deep in our being.
Locked in memories weigh us down.
Last evening a neighbor was visiting.
We've shared before.
We agreed to take turns—
she'd tell an embarrassing secret;
then I'd tell one of mine.
It was striking how parallel our experiences have been,
how similar our feelings were. It was laughable.
Yes, it was—it was laughable!
And that's just what we did. We laughed.
We emptied out our dreaded stories and we laughed.
One story prompted another—
we could hardly wait our turn.
Those buried poisons bubbled to the surface
and burst out in wonderful escape.
It was marvelous.
We've cried together before,
but last night we laughed
over some of our most painful memories.
Imagine!
When she went home, I slept soundly until morning.

ᕉ ᕉ ᕉ

For the first time in my life
I feel a completeness in myself.
A sense of being solid. Whole.
I don't yearn desperately to belong to someone.
I belong to myself and God.
I want to share my life with someone some day,
but my happiness doesn't depend upon it.
I'm free from addiction.
I'm free from feeling helpless and small.
I don't need to attach to someone
who seems to have qualities I lack.
I'm content with myself the way I am.
I have my own activities. I enjoy them.
Some day I might join with someone who is my equal.
Someone who will be my friend.
Someone who is able to love.
Someone who loves himself
and will also love me.
Someone who is happy.
Someone who can give as well as receive.
Someone who wants us both to grow.
We'll each be a complete and independent unit
ready to join together in a healthy relationship.
One flesh joined in God's spirit.
I thank God for my healing.

ે। ે। ે।

Two years have passed since I came to Scandia.
Two amazing years. I am a new person.
My divorce is final, but I still can't believe it.
My dad is gone.
The square brick house and all the contents
were sold at public auction.
Quite the day for me—a panorama of nostalgia
as familiar items were held up for bidding.
It was a graduation day for me,
the end of an era.
I let it all soak in as I watched.
My special friend was there.
A fitting piece—that's where our friendship began.
It was wonderful to see him greet my family again.
They were glad to see him;
they know what he has meant to me.
We have learned so much together.
We've learned that codependence
is not a disease for women only.
Men can be enablers too.
Now it's his turn to tell his story.
Men seem to have a harder time opening up
to release the pain.
Now it's my turn to listen.
I gladly return the favor.
I'm familiar with the process of
denial, confusion, dredging up of memories.

There's no short cut.
Healing takes a lot of time and effort.
I thank God for the privilege of giving encouragement
to this person who is dear to me.
I was thrilled when he came back into my life,
but now to share in his healing process
is a joy beyond words.
I believe it is God's special reward to me
for the wrenching agony I have endured.
The agony of identifying old patterns
and being willing to learn new ones.
The painful struggle of falling back into old ways
until new ones take hold.
God has led me through a process of fire
and I will be grateful forever.
I delight in each new day.
I welcome each new lesson.
I'll share my lessons
with anyone He sends to me.
I no longer fear ridicule.
I present God's help to everyone.
Their response is the only variable.
They must choose to follow Him.
It's the best decision I've ever made.

ðª ðª ðª

For me being a Christian is a way of life.
It is more than going to church.
It is more than being a good person.
Being a Christian means
choosing to follow Christ.
Putting Him first in my life.
Depending on Him for guidance.
Obeying that guidance not knowing the outcome.
Growing.
Being a Christian is
    challenging
       lonely
          frightening
             painful
                exhilarating.
It's a life of suspense, power, sorrow, joy.
A source of peace.
Above all it is a commitment—
    a way of seeing life
      a way of new life
        a new chance each day
          forgiveness.
I believe being a Christian
is the answer to happiness and wholeness.
I embrace it.

ᨀ ᨀ ᨀ

The best part
of being healthy and happy
is listening to young people tell their story.
I love them.
I'm honored that they trust me.
I understand their pain.
I ache for them.
I yearn for their release from locked-in memories.
I want them to escape the prison of their past.
The worst part,
the most frustrating part,
is hearing someone tell about an alcoholic parent
while they draw comfort and courage
from their own glass.
That glass almost screams at me.
It grows in size as they talk.
Danger signals pulsate from it.
I want to grab it!
I want to shout a warning to them.
"Watch out!
Be careful!
I'm afraid you'll be next!"

ہa ہa ہa

I spent last week at a ski lodge.
So what if I don't ski?
There were several significant events.
Since I wasn't skiing,
I began the old "I'm dumb" feelings.
I caught myself and reviewed my lessons.
My attitude would determine my behavior
and probably the response from the others.
As I was pondering my choices,
a hot air balloon floated by. Ta da!
I now proudly display a parchment-like diploma
certifying that this old lady
who's afraid to peer over a balcony rail,
actually ascended into the sky in a basket!
It was great.
Now here's the bad news.
This same lady, with the idea of helping the maid,
put the old towels outside the door.
Communications faltered
and three people air-dried as a result.
I learned through vivid demonstration
that rescuing codependents end up as victims,
and make life difficult for those around them.

ใช้ ใช้ ใช้

I have just read about Jesus calming the storm.
That is exactly what He has done for me.
A storm I didn't even recognize.
A storm I couldn't deal with.
I internalized the pain into years of headaches.
Now in the aftermath, I see the destruction—
the quiet dysfunction.
My ignorance and denial
kept it quiet and kept it going.
I marvel at the way God has revealed truth to me
in gradual doses. Painful treatments
administered with the balm of love.
I see the storm clearly now.
I can finally admit the force of it.
I want to clean up the debris and rebuild.
I must let go of guilt and regret.
I must let go of old patterns,
especially my fear of anger.
Healthy anger and love can exist together.
I can admit my fears.
Having feelings means being vulnerable sometimes.
Being vulnerable is uncomfortable, but not fatal.
Feeling inadequate is human—we all get a turn.
When I panic that I've made a mistake,
I call out to Jesus
who calms my fears once more.

ૐ ૐ ૐ

When I was little,
there was nothing to fill the emptiness.
It was a matter of waiting
and dreaming—
someone would come.
There were no choices,
no options,
no encouragement.
Just emptiness.
Waiting.

I'm not little anymore.
I have resources, choices, opportunities.
I can give myself encouragement.
I have friends—we give each other encouragement.
We understand each other.
We're learning the same lessons.
I have control over my own life.
I set goals and do them.
I'm working toward emotional independence.
I can give to others or say no.
I no longer have an addiction
that keeps me in bondage and cripples others.
I have new patterns at last!

ॐ ॐ ॐ

16　The Big Picture

I am amazed as I listen—
　　men and women pouring out their hearts,
Their voices join in my old song.
We need love so badly,
　　we settle for anything.
We accept scraps
　　because we are starving for love.
We give of ourselves to stark depletion.
We are hollow shells craving to be filled.
Yearning for more, we do too much.
We do not know any better.
We do not know any better.
We are programmed to tolerate neglect.
We don't recognize our part in it.
We do not see our worth.
Out of desperation and ignorance,
　　we actually invite abuse.
We do not know any other way.
But we are beginning to learn another way.
We will sing a new song.

❧　❧　❧

We cannot stand up straight
    and be on our knees at the same time.
We cannot stand erect
    and grovel at someone's feet.
We cannot have self-worth
    and beg for attention.
We cannot respect ourselves
    and accept abuse from others.
These things are incompatible—opposites.
It is a matter of choice—one or the other.
We can choose!
Which shall we choose?
Wholeness or dysfunction?
Are we willing to work on it?
How soon will we get started?
Who will help us?

                    ⅈ ⅈ ⅈ

The fear of the Lord
  is the beginning of wisdom.
Fear in this sense
  does not mean being frightened.
It means awareness—
  accepting God's love,
  recognizing the vast potential of God's power,
  being open to the possibilities for our lives,
  paying attention to guidance.
Men and women who need help
  will get it from the Lord.
The Bible is filled with stories
  to prove that claim.
Men and women who want guidance,
  will get it from the Lord.
The Bible gives clear instructions.
Men are to love their wives
  the same as their own body.
Submission of the wife was meant to
  encourage cooperation not degradation.
Our Lord had respect for women.
The bottom line is this:
  husbands and wives are instructed
  to have mutual respect for each other.

ᏒᎯ ᏒᎯ ᏒᎯ

If I think well of myself,
 I am at peace.
No matter what you say to me,
 I know I am worthwhile.
I won't agree with your insults.
I might not speak up against you,
 but I will not agree inside.
I won't be influenced by your attack.
I will not absorb it—make it part of me.
God's protection shields me.
His love is my covering.
He died for me—He loved me that much.
He came that my joy would be full.
This is quality love.
If God values me, I must be of value.
If I'm valuable and you don't agree,
 you must be mistaken.

 za za za

What is the answer?
What is my cure?
It begins with God.
    Time with him—studying and praying,
    then listening for answers.
Answers come.
    I'll recognize them if I want to obey.
After God's help, comes human help,
    therapists, friends, myself, support groups.
Books and classes.
Practice.
Determination.
And more practice.
When I fall down, slide backwards,
    I start over
        from the beginning.
God.

ᔧ ᔧ ᔧ

If I don't love myself,
    I invite mistreatment.
How?
I simply don't recognize it!
I've been giving neglect to myself
    for so long, it feels normal.
I accept what you give me as normal
    instead of what it really is—
bad treatment.

If I love myself,
    I see the world through different eyes.
I reach out from a steady base.
I give and receive.

If I truly know God's love,
    I am a new person.
I become a healthy person.
I am changed.
God helps me.
My life is a reflection of His love.

            ॐ ॐ ॐ

To be fortunate means to have unexpected joy.
Fortunate are you who know you need God—
    you will surely find Him.
Fortunate are you who are disappointed—
    God will comfort you.
Fortunate are you who feel small—
    you will receive God's strength.
Fortunate are you who try to obey—
    God will lead you.
Fortunate are you who are kind to others—
    God will be kind to you.
Fortunate are you who are simple in heart—
    you will see God in many ways.
Fortunate are you who are well-meaning—
    God will be faithful to you.
Fortunate are you who are criticized for
    obeying the directions you hear—
    The Kingdom of Heaven is real to you.
Remember Moses' words to Joshua.
Put them where you can read them often.
    "Don't be afraid,
    for the Lord will go before you
    and be with you;
    He will not fail nor forsake you." [15]
This is all true—it just takes time to learn.

                ᴈ᙭ ᴈ᙭ ᴈ᙭

I am sitting here while someone
reads what I have written—
the outpouring of my heart, my inmost feelings,
my hardest struggles, my worst pain.
I'm completely vulnerable—there's no turning back.
What will he think?
It is absolutely quiet in this room.
The clock will strike pretty soon.
He's young and strong, this friend of my son.
Will he think I'm crazy?
Will he think I'm a fool?
Will he get in touch with his own feelings?
Will he share with me?
Will he learn that some day he can be free
from the bondage of his past?
I want him to know that it's possible.
I know because I have done it.
I was able to do all of this
because God helped me.
He led me through it all.
He rules the tides, the winds and the waves,
but He has time for me.
He has time for each one of us.

 za za za

Epilogue

Four years have passed since I began these pages. More than five years since I was surrounded by God's cushion of comfort and the awareness that something very painful was going to happen. Something very painful did happen. I could never have guessed what lay ahead nor the severity of the pain. Never had I thought of divorce. Never had I even considered it. It was the furthest thing from my mind.

God moves in amazing ways. I will never doubt that ever again. Anything is possible. The way God led me from one lesson to the next is incredible to me. How my dysfunction was revealed to me in a gradual and systematic way could only have been done by the Master Healer. No human therapist could have scheduled my lessons so skillfully. Encouragement and support were coordinated with my lessons. God is a loving teacher. He knows our hearts and innermost struggles. He knows what has imprisoned us. He knows how threatening it is for us to change.

Since I began these pages, codependence has become a familiar word. Self-defeating behavior like mine is better understood and recognized more quickly. CoDA groups (Codependents Anonymous) have begun.

Ah yes, my dear friend. He is still my dear friend. God has used our relationship to effect individual healing for us both. It has been truly remarkable. I will never stop thanking God for bringing this person back into my life. He has been a blessing for my children as well.

I want to share one more significant thing. When I read

back through my pages, I don't relate to my story any more. I am no longer weary with unmet expectations. I am not struggling with confusion and guilt. I am not intimidated by businessmen and authority figures. I meet each challenge as it comes. Sometimes I wrestle, and I make mistakes. But I can take it in stride. I've learned to be kind to myself.

I thank God for each day of my new healthy life. With Him all things are possible. I am free of the bondage of my past. My early programming does not hold me prisoner anymore. I have new responses. Praise God. He heard me and He had time for me. He always will.

References

The following references are given in case further study is desired. The phrases used in my book are not exact quotations from a single translation.

1.   Deut. 5:7
2.   Ps. 37:4
3.   Eph. 5:22
4.   Ps. 121:1
5.   Eph. 4:26
6.   Lk. 9:48
7.   Matt. 6:13
8.   Matt. 4:4
9.   Rom. 8:28
10.   Deut. 5:9
11.   Ps. 23
12.   Prov. 16:3
13.   Matt. 7:6
14.   John 5:6
15.   Deut. 31:8

Copies of this book may be obtained by sending $9.95
plus $1.50 handling cost. Add $3.00 for handling on two
or more books. In Indiana, add 5% sales tax.

Scandia Press
P.O. Box 501405
Indianapolis, IN 46250-1405

SCANDIA PRESS
8060 CLEARWATER PKWY
INDIANAPOLIS, IN 46240-4903